STRONGMEN

STRONGMEN

Trump ◆ Modi ◆ Erdoğan ◆ Putin ◆ Duterte

Eve Ensler
Danish Husain
Burhan Sönmez
Lara Vapnyar
Ninotchka Rosca

Edited by Vijay Prashad

OR Books
New York · London

All rights information: rights@orbooks.com

Visit our website at www.orbooks.com

First printing 2018.

Published by arrangement with LeftWord Books, New Delhi.

Library of Congress Cataloging-in-Publication Data: A catalog record for this book is available from the Library of Congress.

Typeset by Lapiz Digital Services.
Published for the book trade by OR Books in partnership with Counterpoint Press. Distributed to the trade by Publishers Group West.

hardcover ISBN 978-1-949017-02-1 • ebook ISBN 978-1-949017-03-8

CONTENTS

El odio se ha formado escama a escama,
Golpe a golpe, en el agua terrible del pantano,
Con un hocico ileno de légamo y silencio.

Hatred has grown scale on scale,
Blow on blow, in the ghastly water of the swamp,
With a snout full of ooze and silence.

—Pablo Neruda, "Los Dictadores"

INTRODUCTION
The Return of the Monster

Vijay Prashad

> The crisis consists precisely in the fact that the old is dying
> and the new cannot be born. In this interregnum, a great
> variety of morbid symptoms appear.
>
> —Antonio Gramsci, *Prison Notebooks*, 1930

THE MONSTERS have returned. They are led by strongmen—by Trump, by Modi, by Erdoğan, by Duterte, and by others. But these are not really *strong* men. These are men who pretend to be strong, who hide behind ugly rhetoric that befuddles the masses, but who are nothing other than cowardly when it comes to social reality. Rather than confront the difficult problems that face us— problems of unemployment and starvation, humiliation and inequality—they take refuge in an easy rhetoric of hate. It is so much easier to hate than to spend the time necessary to build the ramparts of a future world, one where the catastrophic social problems of today no longer define human existence. But the monsters of today—the morbid symptoms of this period of transition—do not care to tackle the problems of society. They blink at them, nod at them, and then move on to harsher prescriptions.

At first glance, these monsters appear to be like the fascists of the last century—Germany's Adolph Hitler, Italy's Benito Mussolini, Spain's Francisco Franco, and Japan's Hideki Tojo as well as Portugal's António de Oliveira Salazar, Romania's Ion Antonescu, and South Africa's D.F. Malan. These men and their regimes are defined by the ugliness of their political agendas as well as their rhetoric—bilious against social groups that they abhor. Violence is both their strategy and their tactic. The current monsters even resemble the monsters of the 1960s and the 1970s, the men who led the neo-fascist states through the military *juntas* (Argentina, Brazil, Chile, Greece, Indonesia, and Thailand); these were weak states that used force to extract resources at low prices for export and to produce markets for high value imported goods—all at the behest of multinational corporations and imperial centers.

But the current monsters are a shadow of the older fraternity. They do not advertise themselves as fascists, neither wearing the same emblems nor using the same rhetoric. Some of their followers carry swastikas on their signs, but most of them are more careful. They do not wear the uniform of the military, nor indeed call the military out of the barracks to lend them a hand. Their fascism is couched in modern rhetoric—in the terms of development or trade, in the terms of jobs and social welfare for their nationals, in the language of threats from migrants and drug gangs. But the older language of the older monsters cannot stay away. It makes its appearance when the new monsters speak of migrants and of the vulnerable, of the social and political dissidents. They are treated as vermin that need to be exterminated. The military comes to the border or goes into the slums, bullets flying. Dislocation of society is their goal. Older, decadent language can be heard, the language of death and disorder.

◆

Why have the monsters returned? They made their appearance in the West in the 1920s and 1930 when the workers' movement had asserted itself and when capitalism went into a tailspin. At that time, the monsters came to suffocate the workers' movement and to steady the capitalist ship. They broke up the parties of the Left and absorbed a section of the workers into their outfits. They attacked society, attacked its institutions and its confidence— leaving the militant workers of the Left vulnerable. The monsters, "swollen with rhetoric" as Gramsci put it, chastised society for its desire for a better world. Intimidation was the order of things, the fulcrum upon which the monsters were able to balance their own will to power with the desire to produce a social order to advantage big business. But even the capitalist had to appear to face their wrath. They took the capitalists into a room and scolded them for being insufficiently patriotic to capitalism. The *class* of capitalists had to protect capitalism against their individual capitalist interests. The monsters arrived to save capitalism from the militancy of the workers and the cupidity of the capitalists.

The monsters told people to fear their minions, the men who marched in ironed uniforms and with polished jackboots. If anyone strayed from the norm, the men in boots would descend on them. These fascists were the detritus of a decadent capitalism.

3

Their ambitions were destroyed in the fires of war, their project compromised by their disgusting violence against humanity.

That was then; this is now. Why have these monsters returned?

These days, the workers' movement is weak, debilitated by ideology and technology—by the lure of commodities and by the productivity of computers. Left parties are few, and if they exist, they are weakened by the difficulties of organizing the workers, the peasants, and the unemployed—the key classes who spend so much more time on social reproduction, on finding work, and on travelling to work than they ever did. Individual advancement as an ideological platform is an overwhelming barrier to collective projects of the Left. There is no immediate danger to capitalism in that direction. Bourgeois democracy is fully capable of draining the reservoirs of the Left. The capitalist class does not *need* fascism for this purpose. If fascists appear, it is not because the Left is a threat to the capitalists.

But capitalism itself is in disarray. Inequality rates are astounding. It is as if the very rich, of whom there are fewer and fewer, are of a different breed than the very poor—of whom there are more and more. A thick and high wall has divided humanity. The poor imagine that they could become rich if luck struck them, but they know that the chances of this are minuscule. The rich, in turn, know that they will never be poor again. They have accumulated generations of wealth by taking advantage of the gibberish of the world of finance, the New Science, the new vocabulary of the alchemists of money: BISTRO, CDS, CDO, CDOs of ABSs, CDOs of CDOs, CDOs of CDOs of CDOs, RAROC, SCDOs, SIVs, SPOs, and VAR. Money makes money, financial instruments insure that the wealthy remain wealthy and that pension funds and middle-class investors feed the system to the advantage of the rich. The house always wins say those who run casinos. Financial exchanges, oxygenated by petro-dollars and derivatives, always favor the wealthy. The rich have withdrawn their wealth—to the tune of trillions of dollars—from either investment or from taxation, although they plow it into financial instruments that do little productive good for the economy. The rich are hoarding the wealth produced by the workers. They have weakened the economic system: its arteries are dry, its heart ready to seize. A small heart attack of the financial system in 2007-08 took place when the US housing market failed, and it set off convulsions across the system. Doctors have panicked. Other organs are in danger of failure. Next time, the heart of capitalism might fail altogether.

The monsters have returned because the masters of the New Science have not been able to manage the economy, the free-fall of inequality and humiliation. It is not that the workers and the unemployed workers are now stronger. They are weaker and more disorganized. But they are also angry. And anger can lead in many directions. It can tear society apart, drawing the bile of the torn social structure into family life and into inter-personal relations. It can create anti-social feelings that erupt in violence of all kinds, disassociations from community, hatred of class enemies. The atmosphere of rebellion can always exist without any real possibility of rebellion. Trade unions have been gutted, rural workers have been disinherited from their small plots of land, debt stalks ordinary people from one end of the world to the other, and Left parties are on the back foot. But anger remains. It festers. It could turn into aggression. It could threaten the lives of the rich—their homes on fire, their businesses smashed.

Johann Rupert, the boss of Cartier, told the *Financial Times* Business of Luxury Summit in Monaco in 2015, "How is society going to cope with structural unemployment and the envy, hatred and social warfare? We are destroying the middle classes at this stage and it will affect us. It's unfair. So that's what keeps me awake at night." Nick Hanauer, who made billions of dollars when he sold aQuantive to Microsoft in 2007, wrote to his "fellow Zillionaires" a few years ago. His warning is stark: "No society can sustain this kind of rising inequality. In fact, there is no example in human history where wealth accumulated like this and the pitchfork didn't eventually come out. You show me a highly unequal society, and I will show you a police state. Or an uprising." These are not radicals. These are the people who exist in the realm of the .01 percent of the wealthy. They can see that economic ruin and social humiliation might produce the strongman, but his appearance does not settle the deep sense of resentment and anger amongst the people produced by social conditions generated by a policy that benefits the rich.

Who will keep the workers and the unemployed workers in line and capitalism humming? The monsters. That is why they have returned. Not to attack the workers' movement, because it is weak and is not an immediate threat, but to remove the gloves and crack down on collapsed society. Security states grow, the police are in charge, and militia groups emerge to intimidate society into silence. Lynchings of Dalits and Muslims in India are linked to the murder of supposed drug dealers in the Philippines, who are further linked to the shooting of black men and women by police officers in the United States. The monsters take their cue from normal, boring bourgeois democracy. The institutions of bourgeois democracy are also saturated with the apparatus of repression. You don't need the monsters for police brutality to become normal or for wars to distract you from your own problems. But the monsters offer something more. They are not just bourgeois democrats who hide behind the police and the military. They are out on the streets, telling the hemorrhaging middle-class and the unemployed workers that it is neither the rich nor the state apparatus that are to blame for social failure. Nor is the way ahead for the despondent white-collar and blue-collar worker the path of the entrepreneur. The way ahead is to disparage the marginal, the vulnerable. It is those people who are at fault.

The monsters return not to tell the capitalists to pay more tax, but certainly to tell them to invest more. The monsters grab the economy by the throat and force it to cough out jobs. Yes, they are able to discipline the workers and the unemployed workers. But they cannot force the rich to produce jobs. That will not happen. Millions of people are no longer going to find employment. They have been made into zombies—the living dead. They exist so that they will soon not exist; they are born, but purpose has been taken from their lives. But what to do with their anger?

It is to be displaced, to be reoriented. Why should the workers and the unemployed workers worry about the rich? After all, say the monsters, the rich have earned their wealth. It is by ingenuity and hard work that the rich have climbed to the summit and built a gated community around their house. They have dug a moat around their community and erected guard towers with drones in flight between them. Anger at the rich will only get you killed, say the monsters. Don't target the rich, they say. Turn your guns against the socially marginal.

The old monsters had a clever idea. They turned the workers and the unemployed workers as well as the middle-class against the Reds—who helped the workers remain strong—but also against the homosexuals and the Jews. It was easy to target the homosexuals, for there had been centuries of animosity bred inside religious traditions for anything that did not conform to the most conservative definition of human relations. It was even easier to target the Jews. Modern capitalism is bewildering, modern finance capitalism even more so. In the old days, the angry peasants would attack the home of the landlord or the overseers or the moneylender. They would run across the fields, pitchforks raised and torches lit. They knew who oppressed them. Matters were reasonably easy in the early days of industrial capitalism, when the factory was the target of the workers' anger.

But with finance the game is difficult. Who is there to attack, which field to cross, which house to set on fire? Finance capital dominates through the structure, anonymously, a stealth form of oppression. The workers and the unemployed workers know that they are oppressed and exploited and made disposable. They know all this. But what they don't easily know is who is responsible for their situation. They cannot burn down the bank, because the bank is not one building—there are too many branches, too many ATMs. They cannot burn down the corporate office, because they know that there are many of these as well, in many countries. The old monsters pointed their fingers at the Jews— there is your financier they said, using the deeply rooted language of anti-Semitism. The pogroms against the Jews morphed into the gas chambers of Auschwitz and Treblinka.

The new monsters borrow the old monster's idea. Workers and unemployed workers, the disposable part of humanity, also look at capitalism and wonder at who is firing them, who has ruined their lives. Once in a while, a disgruntled worker takes a gun to his former workplace and shoots his former boss. This happens. But not as often as you'd imagine. The guns are mostly turned against strangers, the rage phantasmagorical. The new monsters point their fingers elsewhere, away from the rich and the powerful and towards the vulnerable and the weak. It is the migrant that gets the brunt of the blame, for it is said—against all the facts—that it is the migrant who is taking away jobs from the workers and the unemployed workers. The migrants come from places of great desperation, where they have seen their own fields torn apart by capitalist farming and their jobs as landless workers vanished by mechanization. They have travelled across the deserts and waters at great peril, risking life and limb to get to places where they think they will find better work. There are few options for them in the new lands, where they find themselves doing the butt-end jobs and being treated with contempt by the armies raised by the new monsters. It is the migrant who must suffer for the plight of the workers and the unemployed workers. The migrants are the sacrifice for capitalism's failure.

If it is not the migrant who is to blame, then it is some other social figure—the drug dealer or the terrorist. Citizenship is denied to them, the protections of basic human rights are withdrawn. Martial law arrives. Emergency powers are enacted. The strong-man must be allowed latitude to protect the *real* citizens from those who have violated the framework of citizenship. There is no gap between the terrorist or the drug dealer and the migrant— even as the liberal might plead that the migrant is a victim of circumstance and not of choice. These liberal distinctions vanish at the heel of the state's boot.

It is this hatred of the migrant, the terrorist, and the drug dealer—all seen equally as sociopaths—that evokes an acerbic form of nationalism, a nationalism that is not rooted in love of one's fellows but in hatred of the outsider. Hatred masquerades as patriotism. The size of the national flag grows, the enthusiasm for the national anthem increases by decibels. Patriotism is reduced to hatred of the migrant, the terrorist, and the drug dealer. It smells acrid—of anger and bitterness, of violence and frustration. The eyes of the workers and the unemployed workers as well as sections of the middle class are turned away from their own problems, from the low wages and the near starvation in their homes, from lack of educational opportunities and provisions for health care, to other problems, problems that are false, that are invented by the new monsters to turn them away from their real problems. It is one thing to be patriotic about flags and anthems. But it is another thing to be patriotic against starvation and hopelessness. The new monsters have taken the second kind of patriotism and thrown it into the fire. Human beings ache to be decent. But that ache is smothered by desperation and resentment, by the diabolical new monsters.

◆

This small book is a collection of fables.

Five brilliant artists and writers confront five of our monsters. Eve Ensler, the American playwright who wrote the play *The Vagina Monologues*, goes beneath the skin—or should I say orange hair—of US President Donald Trump. Danish Husain, the Indian storyteller and actor, finds himself telling us the story not only of Indian Prime Minister Narendra Modi but also of the ascension of the extremism of the Sangh Parivar. Burhan Sönmez, the Turkish novelist, ferrets about amidst the bewildering career of the Turkish President Recep Tayyip Erdoğan. Ninotchka Rosca, the Filipina feminist novelist, unravels the macho world of Rodrigo Duterte. And Lara Vapnyar, Russian-American novelist and essayist, lays bare the sinister sexiness of Vladimir Putin.

There are many other monsters that could have made it into these pages. This is not a comprehensive list, just a suggestive one. We encourage people to write their own essays. In fact, please write them and send them to me (vijay@leftword.com). We will post them on our LeftWord Books blog, http://mayday.leftword.com/blog/.

But, for now, settle in and read these five superb essays by these sparkling writers. Their essays do not presume to be neutral. They are partisan thinkers, magical writers, people who see not only the monsters but also a future beyond the ghouls. A future that is necessary. The present is too painful.

TRUMP
A Fable

Eve Ensler

THIS IS THE STORY of what happened in the late time, right before the end time, that later got interrupted and became the new time. In those days there arrived in the land of violent amnesia and rapacious dreams—a virus. It first became discernible in an oafish, chubby man with orange hair. Some say it was the virus that turned his hair orange. Others claimed his hair was actually the virus. The oafish, chubby man with orange hair goes on to become the most powerful man in the world.

It was highly debated whether the intensity of the infection was the cause of his rise, but it has since become clear that the virus was a very contagious one and that much of the populace had a dormant strain of it lodged in their beings which was activated by the orange man during his toxic campaign.

Those infected the most deeply were those with unexamined wounds and openings from childhood, repressed fear, insecurities that were ripe for othering and rage, predisposition towards racism and sexism and insatiable daddy hunger. These tendencies were exacerbated and catalyzed by the way the portly, thuggish leader

13

injected the virus into the unsuspecting crowds through angry
white-hate filled spittle, slimy superlatives, sham-filled promises,
and toxic red caps which allowed the virus to seep in through the
hair follicles and head. Bald men were most susceptible.

This, fortunately, was not true of all segments of the population because some appeared to have built-in immunity. Most of
those were the ones who lived on the various edges, which was
ironic, as it was the ones most foreign and exiled from the culture
who would eventually find a cure. We will come to that later.

It was also highly debated whether the man with orange
hair was the origin of the virus or simply the manifestation of it.
Some said it didn't matter, but I believe it matters a lot. For if
the chubby man were the originator of the virus, then it would
have simply been one sick individual contaminating the public
and if and when he was eliminated, the virus, would, in theory,
be gone as well. But we know this didn't happen. So the question
then evolved: why was the oafish, portly man with orange hair the
major host of the virus?

And again, the theories abound.

One classic theory is that the thuggish man had become what
no one had yet become in the time of late date consumption and
greed. He had evolved or devolved (depending on your perspec-
tive) into what the psychologists later came to define as a **genocidal narcissist**—*a person willing and able to destroy everyone
and everything on the planet as long as it makes him feel momen-
tarily better.* That extreme and total endgame narcissism made
the oafish man a perfect super host for the virus. For it has since
been discovered that the virus can only fester in an environment
where the host has developed no antibodies to tolerate others,

14

or indeed criticism, difference, curiosity, questions, doubt, ambiguity, the truth, mystery, waiting, thinking, reading, reflecting, questioning, wondering, caring, feeling, listening, or studying. It is where the healing properties of humor and irony have been killed off and self-obsession, revenge, and self-adulation have taken their place.

Noted symptoms of the virus are: hysteria, mania, illogical thinking, impulse disorder, bullying, a distorted belief that the group and gender to which you belong is superior, vile and show-offy compulsive grabbing, molesting behavior towards women, compulsive lying, increased paranoia, loss of ability to distinguish between good and evil (for example equating Nazis and white supremacists with people fighting for their constitutional rights), and shifting and constantly evolving enemies, because the infection needs a target to energize its effective components. One day it was Mexicans, the next day blonde women reporters, the next a Puerto Rican mayor, the next black football players. It was actually irrelevant to the virus who the enemy was as long as it kept shifting and escalating as the pathogen craved and fed off this antagonistic energy. But it has been conclusively determined that the virus would first seek already existing weaknesses in the DNA of the culture.

If, for example, the culture had never addressed or healed from historical and on-going oppressions, genocides, or hatreds, the virus could easily attach itself to these previous maladies and multiply as the virus thrives on unexamined, pustulating moral wounds.

There have been many studies done into the roots of the infection. Historians, political scientists, Marxists, business leaders, race scholars, eco-feminists, bacteriologists, philosophers, pathologists, and artists each offered various theories and hypothesis. It was believed for quite some time in some religious quarters, those that believe in other lifetimes, that the virus was a kind of karma *extremis*, a poisonous accumulation of the terrible deeds done by the orange man's empiric nation of Coca-Cola. That the original genocidal acts committed against the native people, the hundreds of years of slavery and hatred and systemic racism, the concurring years of unfettered economic growth hinged on endless murder, rape, pillaging, and war, invasions, land mines, napalm, nuclear bombs, destruction of the earth, hatred of workers, simply flooded the collective psychic basin and tore through the membrane that acts as protective spiritual ozone for humanity. This cosmic tear rendered the most shallow, unreflective, fearful, angry, and bitter totally vulnerable to the noxious strain. It was believed by some that the rotund man was actually not a man at all, but an orange demonic entity.

But there were many who had always seen capitalism as a producer of a parallel chronic and deadly virus, one of low self-esteem created by the eternal pressure of the competitive machine and colonizing forces of branding. They saw the chunky mean orange man as the ultimate purveyor of carcinogenic comparison and suicidal self-hatred. He had, through trickster practices convinced the people that he was the modern-day king of monopoly, that singular individual who had managed to erect phallic gold towers in many cities and have his name plastered across the universe. He was what was called in those days a **huge** success and it was believed that it was the unlikely and extreme combination of envy and awe that had propelled him to the top. The fact that no one was able to really determine if he was a **huge** success (as his tax returns were never made available) seemed bizarrely irrelevant to his followers, as did the many cases he had declared of bankruptcy. Fantasy carried the day, an incurable strain of delusional devotional father fever. It was astounding to see how long this fever persisted.

Then there were the environmentalists, mycologists, biologists, botanists, entomologists, geneticists, herpetologists, ichthyologists, neuroscientists, and many others who were actually in agreement that climate change was at the core of the virus, because it had a less direct but definite effect on infectious diseases. Climate and weather alterations impacted viruses and the animal and insects that host them and could radically change how humans were exposed. During the time of the orange man, for example, the world had seen radical increases in childhood learning disabilities, ADD, autism, Lyme disease, depression, anxiety, and suicide of teenagers and even a return of the bubonic plague. All of these were directly linked to environmental damage. So it was wildly agreed that the virus hosted by the orange man was caused by extreme pollution of some sort—air, the loss of coral reefs, pesticides, warming of the seas, or a combination thereof.

There was a whole school of acarologists in Massachusetts who had serious data proving that the virus was linked with the "nine iron tick," a nine-legged arachnid only found on golf courses buried deep in sand traps. It was the conjecture of the acarologists that the parasitic properties of the tick were transmuted into the host and that he in turn fed off the blood of the people he infected.

The oncologists had a very different reading and believed the virus was a tumor-causing agent and was somehow related to diminishing testosterone, which manifested as a brain lesion/ tumor rendering the host or infected one into a violent fool. It is not clear whether the tumor made the host violent or being a fool made him violent or if they were one and the same. The tumor, constantly pressing on the brain, created a sense in the host that he was always under surveillance which is why he despised the press and the former leader of the land who he constantly accused, without a drop of evidence, of surveilling him. The orange idiot would have constant mad outbursts of this violence on something at the time called Twitter, a bizarre technological mechanism that shot word pellets into the public.

And, there was evidence that this virus was spreading and worsening. It began appearing in other men who were suddenly going on shooting rampages, murdering hundreds at concerts and shopping malls and other public gatherings with no apparent motives. It became known after many of these incidents that white men over the age of fifty were the main carriers of the disease as they had not, due to privilege and arrogance, developed the necessary and flexible antibodies mentioned above to fight off the virus.

This enraged a powerful community of feminists who thought little of the virus theory. They were thoroughly convinced that the so-called virus was not a virus at all but the final manifestation of malignant racist patriarchy. They were disturbed that it was being called a virus as it took responsibility from the rotund oinker with orange hair and all his followers and made it seem like something they had caught rather than something they were perpetrating. But even some amongst them had to admit that the qualities, persistence, and recurrence of racist patriarchy made it seem much like a virus, and they were still at a loss to explain how thousands of white women had voted for the chubby gangster after he had bragged about being able to grab their pussy parts because he was famous.

There were many women who believed the orange round slime was no longer a man at all, but through the deteriorating impact of the virus had become a kind of octopus, (not to insult octopi as they are highly-evolved creatures). Yes, they thought he had become a soft-bodied, eight-armed mollusk whose flaccid body could rapidly alter its shape and whose many groping tentacles would sometimes, at parties, on airplanes, or during job interviews, travel up women's skirts attempting to get through their panties or into their blouses, sliding and ejecting a dark goo around their breasts. These mushy octopi seemed to replicate throughout the land. They would station themselves at the head of entertainment and news companies where they would incubate for years and were able to easily shoot their goo and wrap their tentacles around hundreds of women in broad daylight while other men with low-level infection, awed by the octopi, longing for similar position and fortune, watched and said nothing.

Some saw the octopi as the ultimate performer in a culture hinged on fantasy and entertainment. They blamed the TV executives for the original spread of the virus as from the onset the corporate leaders understood that the vicious carrot man increased their ratings and sold more Subarus. The populace was glued to the corpulent con artist with an all-consuming fascination that verged on obsession. Because they had long ago lost the ability to distinguish the real from unreal they were transfixed by the on-going sideshow, somehow disconnected from the catastrophic outcome.

And there were a small group who believed the nation had simply been seized by a scary clown and that the population was suffering from coulrophobia, a **fear** of clowns that rendered people paralyzed, terrified, anxious, and dysfunctional. The man with the orange hair smiled when he was murderous, he told lies by the minute, and committed crimes daily. Like the notorious John Wayne Gacy, a clown who was actually a serial killer who had murdered thirty-three people, he understood, as Gacy said, "Clowns can get away with anything."

Then there were those who kept believing the virus would pass, that it was only momentary, and that it couldn't possibly hold or spread further. They were sure it was simply a strange aberration that would never be tolerated and if they did not give it attention, it would disappear. These are the same people who feel a bump under their skin or see blood in their poop and believe that if they ignore it really, really hard, it will somehow go away. It is hard to tell whether these folks had actually already been infected by the virus, as one of the major symptoms of the virus was an inability to know that you have it.

Another major component of the virus that ravaged privileged people was their refusal to resist it. The privileged were simply unable to give up their daily comforts in order to fight the virus when it began to infect and destroy the lives of the less fortunate. The virus created a superstitious delusion in them that if they did not focus on the virus they couldn't catch it. If rather than ignoring it, if they looked at it or touched it—the privileged truly believed—they would get it. This delusion later proved to be fatal.

Then there were those who could perceive the virus and who should have been actively fighting it. They were called *liberalatte*.

Because no one in this group was practiced in telling the whole truth, because they were an opposition that had ceased being the opposition years ago, they tried to placate the virus, adapt to the virus, and accommodate the virus. For some inexplicable reason they seemed worried about offending the virus and therefore making it worse. The virus would occasionally ruffle the liberalatte, but they had lost the will or the energy to scream out for all the millions who were suffering from the deep sickness the virus was spreading.

Because secretly the liberalatte believed that to truly revolt against the virus would alienate the people in the middle, and they were most concerned about losing their positions and power and comfort, they learned how to mute their outrage, sorrow and reactions and by doing so normalized the virus which allowed it to spread wider and deeper.

Then, of course, there were those who served in the court of the orange man. They had contracted the virus and most definitely understood the devastating impact of the virus, and secretly despised the orange octopi pig, but somehow through their malevolence attempted to use the pathogen to their own end. Rather than trying to protect their fellow citizens and stop the deadly virus or disrobe the orange haired emperor, they rode his mad sickness like a wild horse gaining every benefit they could. While the population was being deported, banned, attacked, starved, refused medical treatment, lied to, forced to have babies, run over by cars, shot by police and white supremacists, abandoned, and forced to drink poisoned water after a storm, they moved to get as much money, land, drilling rights, private airplane trips, island vacations, monument parks, tax cuts for themselves as they possibly could. They were called virus bankers.

The malady spread deeper and deeper throughout the land. Crops withered. Fires burned. Storms raged. Animals disappeared. Hate festered and hate crimes escalated.

Generals were hired to police the orange idiot and contain the sickness, but they quickly fell by the wayside, becoming apologists for the plague and its host, losing their integrity and minds. They, of course, had latent aspects of the virus embedded in their own consciousness and began to sound more insane and demented than the tubby lout they were monitoring.

Psychiatrists and psychologists broke protocol and issued warnings to the public that a malignant normality was spreading through the land and that the orange man was insane, living in his own reality, that the people would be unable to manage the crises that would eventually face the most powerful man in the world.

There were many brave determined people who did not have the virus but suffered from its consequences and they rose in the millions in the streets, in the Congress, at airports to prevent the virus from completely ruining their lives. Initially, they were not able to prevent the virus, but their on-going activity kept them from being contaminated themselves.

Committees were formed to investigate the multiple crimes and offenses of the orange fool and the sick people around him.

Some in the press became almost obsessed with reporting on the viscous pestilence almost to the point of orange madness.

Lawyers pressed hundreds of legal cases. Bacteriologists developed sprays and poisons. Pharmacologists harnessed new antibiotics and mood-altering drugs.

Many in the land became hopeless, depressed, suicidal, homicidal, disassociated, hostile, alcoholic. Those who could afford it went shopping or fled to other countries. But the virus followed them there as it had taken hold in new forms and had possessed leaders far and wide.

Arguments raged about methods and tactics of approaching the plague and the orange emperor. The strident ones believed that only complete annihilation would rid the world of the illness. The non-violent practitioners and faith leaders called for empathy and the need for reconciliation, understanding, and healing. They believed if they could unlock the roots of the virus, it could be released from the collective cells. They held vigils and prayer ceremonies and developed spiritual antidotes.

Witches made potions from strands of orange hair and spittle and did ongoing hexes.

But still the virus raged deeper and deeper. The orange followers became so toxic that, although they could feel the impact, they were unable to admit that their jobs, homes, air, water, health care, were being systematically destroyed by their fearless leader. The genocidal narcissist began to prepare them for nuclear Armageddon. This shockingly felt more relieving than the opioids they were addicted to, and less expensive.

The land of violent amnesia and rapacious dreams was nearing its end.

Then something wondrous and surprising began to happen.

The seers, the mystics, the sexual explorers, the artists, the exiles, began to do what they had wanted to do all along, but were now free to do with the end of the world in sight.

They made each other laugh and rubbed and healed each other with special oils and rituals and prayers. They lay with each other and shared their dreams. They listened to each other's stories and made amends and reparations. They learned to read the stars and listen to the wind. They rediscovered ecstasy and poetry and purpose. They grieved for the world and held each other as they wept. They wrapped themselves around trees and bowed down to the rivers. They spent their days dancing and massaging each other. They foraged for food and fed each other. They stopped competing and striving.

Every day was filled with extraordinary acts of kindness. And a warm and delicious energy began to rise. It was liquid like honey and its pull was irresistible. One by one people began to join them. Even those who thought they didn't know how to dance suddenly heard and moved to new rhythms. Even those afraid to touch or be touched found themselves lathering on oils. And a new world began to grow. It was magical and even work seemed like play.

The orange moron became louder and more hysterical but the people could no longer hear him as the radiant music was sweeping across the land. And as his idolaters were transformed into revellers and there was no one to admire or worship him, the people of the land watched with horror and awe as the gross sac of the vile emperor's body began to wither like a deflated orange ball.

And so the moral of the story and the lesson from the orange idiot is to keep your souls clean. Viruses are always lurking but they cannot thrive where the people have washed their past darkness and have fortified themselves with solidarity, imagination, and love.

MODI

The Vanity of the Tyrant

Danish Husain

BABUR STANDS GUARD at dawn outside the newly constructed Taj Mahal in Agra. He dreams of flying palanquins, which he calls *aeroplats*. Babur is with his co-guard Humayun. They are characters in a play I directed in early 2017 called *Guards at the Taj* by Rajiv Joseph. At some point in the play, Babur and Humayun realize that they have a terrible task ahead of them. As menial guards, they must implement the fierce royal decree that says that after the Taj Mahal has been built all those who built it—the twenty thousand labourers, the masons, and even the architect—must have their hands chopped off. This Babur and Humayun do.

Babur dreams that his beloved aeroplats are weapons of destruction in the hands of the enemies of Hindustan. He imagines that they are used by the enemy to attack his country. When the aeroplats fly over Hindustan, they identify it by the shining Taj Mahal. They decide to destroy the mausoleum. The emperor, recognizing the enemy's plan, tells his army to take hold of a large black cloth, run fast enough so that the cloth billows, and then cover the Taj Mahal beneath the cloth. The men—including Babur—run to the cloth, but when they reach it, they realize that most of them cannot hold the cloth. They have no hands. Thus, they stand mute, witnessing the destruction of the Taj Mahal.

"Development" is the Taj Mahal that was sold to the people of India in the 2014 elections. Hindutva is the sword that is now chopping off the hands of the people of this country. We now live *en masse* within this strange twist of fate in Babur's dream. But this is a twist of fate that has a terrible history. The history requires a mirror. The citizens of our country will find that they are partly responsible for our present. We have been complacent. We have not held our representatives accountable. We have kept silent and happily lived on the blinkered dreams our leader threw over us for the past seventy years. We have no hands to hold the cloth. We are spectators to the destruction of our Taj Mahal.

Jumla

My story and acting career coincide with Narendra Modi's ascendency to power. In fact, Modi had a head start on me. He already had a massacre under his watch before I started massacring characters on the stage. In 2002, we both arrived at our current *avatars*. I resigned from my bank job to become an actor. Modi, who had been party to the terrible state-sanctioned pogrom in Gujarat against Muslims in 2002, won an election to lead the government in Gujarat. Modi saw this victory as endorsement by the public of his deeds—including his misdeeds.

Modi is not the first political leader who has seen his electoral victory as redemption, as a referendum on his past. Even if the election victory was secured by manipulation or by rigging the discourse, it was still sufficient to whitewash—or in Modi's case, saffron-wash—his actions. Modi, born in 1950, was just out of his teens when Indira Gandhi won a thumping election victory in 1971—which was seen as vindication of her unfavourable policies and of the reasons for her expulsion from the Congress Party in 1969. The delusion of her victory led us to suffer through the National Emergency for almost two years between 1975 and 1977. Dangerous misuse of tragic events would occur when the Congress Party won a conclusive victory at the polls in 1984 *after* the army had been sent into the Golden Temple in Amritsar, after the assassination of Indira Gandhi and after the murder of three thousand Sikhs. Modi—in a similarly twisted way—used his electoral victory in Gujarat in 2002 as a public approval of the massacre that took place under his watch. Modi understood that power could only be captured through an overpowering narrative and that often such narratives are built on the blood of the dispensable enemy—the "other." He learned his lessons well during the years of his apprenticeship both in the fascistic Rashtriya Swayamsevak Sangh (RSS) and as a careful observer of Indian politics.

Today, both Modi and I are in the middle of our careers. I, as an artist, and he, as a man who attempts to become a myth. We both search for a lasting legacy. But, unlike me, he's almost reached his goal.

The 2014 parliamentary election saw one political party—for the first time since 1984—win an absolute majority. Modi, with his excellent PR campaign and a successful social media campaign like Barack Obama, convinced people that he is pro-development and pro-good governance; he also convinced the business elite that he is their close friend. It was not easy to prove that he was friendly to the business elites. They are his first constituency. The magic of his myth was that he was able to convince people that he was pro-development—a word that still carries enormous meaning for people who wither under poverty and indignity. Every person who has studied Modi closely has been wary of his "success" as the chief minister of Gujarat. The electorate, nonetheless, seemed exhausted by the corrupt incumbent Congress government and was generous towards Modi and his team. But, in the midst of his five-year term, Modi seems to be running out of steam. Most of his election promises have turned out to be empty talk—*jumla*—a rhetorical statement made for an immediate teetering effect with no intention to produce policy and then actual improvements in people's lives. Many of his policy decisions—demonetization and the Goods and Services Tax (GST)—have been duds. Job creation is the slowest it has been in the past seven years. The economy slips downwards. Economists now predict that even massive government spending to boost demand would not help. Social divisions are sharp. Environmental disaster is before us as the air is unbreathable and the soil is polluted each day. The agrarian crisis escalates and food insecurity has allowed the epidemic of hunger to breed across the country. Civil liberties and the freedom of speech are being curtailed. A general sense of unrest prevails.

Modi cannot peddle fiction anymore. Nor can he throw statistics at us. Nor can his grandstanding and event management save him further. Modi is in a desperate search for his legacy.

Farid ud-din Attar's poem "The Simurgh" ("The Conference of the Birds") tells the story of a band of thirty birds who are in search of a king. They cannot find the king. The hoopoe leads them to a lake. They peer into its waters and find themselves—the

28

thirty birds, the *si murgh*. They are what they have been seeking. Modi prances about like the king. But the people won't see themselves in him. If they did for a moment, it was their delusion. They will eventually find themselves. Modi, who they had thought was the *Simurgh*, is an imposter. His legacy is *jumla*.

Origins

When Modi first appeared on the stage, I hardly noticed him. India, by the 1990s, was a great tragedy—*Hamlet* being played in a theater of tattered grandeur. Modi seemed like Rosencrantz or Guildenstern, brought in to distract India from the madness of poverty and religious violence that had torn apart our society. People do not take notice of stardom—or tragedy—until it looms large in their faces.

Modi was a minor figure in Gujarat who caught the attention of his party, the Bharatiya Janata Party (BJP), when he organized party leader Lal Krishna Advani's Rath Yatra through Gujarat in 1990. That Rath Yatra, pickled in hatred and saturated in blood, animated sections of India to assert bilious ideas that had been set aside by our freedom movement: ideas of Hindu assertion, of hatred towards Muslims, and of the normalcy of gender and caste hierarchy. Modi was the producer of the Gujarat version of his Bollywood-like tragedy.

Modi's rise through the BJP in the 1990s was helped along by the deep respect he had earned in the RSS. He used the RSS and its methods to gallop to the front of the BJP's ranks, to become, by 1988, the BJP general secretary in charge of the party's organization. Modi, even by then, was clearly the paragon of the RSS ideology, with a dash of narcissism thrown in on the side. It is not for nothing that the psychologist and social scientist Ashis Nandy called Modi a "fascist" after he interviewed him in his nobody days. Nandy wrote that he did not use this term to abuse Modi, but it was used to describe the symptomatic manifesto of an authoritative mind that was seeped in fascist ideology.

Nothing about Modi is easy to take at face value. The myth has been created by fantasy and by money, more than by reality. It is fitting that Lance Price, the author of *The Spin Doctor*, wrote one of the biographies of Modi. Price said that he had never heard of Modi before the 2014 elections. An anonymous person gave him an undisclosed amount to write *The Modi Effect*, a book that cultivated the Modi myth. It was important to Modi's spin-doctors that the "pen for hire" comes from the United Kingdom—their fascination with validation by the British is part of their legacy. It is what muddled their own ultra-nationalism, whose roots are not so much in our freedom movement as they are in collaboration with imperialism.

Savarkar

V.D. Savarkar (1883-1966) was the architect of Hindutva (Hinduness), the ideology of the RSS and the BJP. This Hindutva was neither comfortable with Indian anti-colonial nationalism nor was it uncomfortable with British imperial rule. Savarkar's own career began with anti-colonial actions, but ended with anti-national politics. He would set the groundwork for the RSS and the BJP and for Modi's peculiar mix of ultra-nationalism in close fealty to the United States and to multinational corporations. In their world, this duality is not unusual. It is the essence of their ideology.

Young Savarkar went to England to study law in 1906. In London, he founded the Free India Society with other Indian students. Three years later, Savarkar was arrested for being an accomplice in the assassination of the Collector of Nasik, A.M.T. Jackson. He was said to have supplied the pistol that killed Jackson. Savarkar was sent to the dreaded Cellular Jail in the Andaman Islands for fifty years. Within the first month of his imprisonment, Savarkar wrote a mercy petition to the British, asking for forgiveness. This was rejected in 1911. He wrote many of these mercy petitions—each in the British archives—each more craven towards the British, each offering his unflinching loyalty to the British Raj. In one of his last mercy petitions, Savarkar wrote,

> If the Government wants a further security from me then I and my brother are perfectly willing to give a pledge of not participating in politics for a definite and reasonable period that the Government would indicate . . . This or any pledge, e.g., of remaining in a particular province or reporting our movements to the police for a definite period after our release—any such reasonable conditions meant genuinely to ensure the safety of the State would be gladly accepted by me and my brother.

After much cajoling and pleading, Savarkar was transferred to a prison on the Indian mainland in 1921, and then he was released in 1924. In prison, Savarkar wrote *Essentials of Hindutva* (1923) and then, out of prison, he wrote his manifesto—*Hindutva: Who is a Hindu?* (1928). In this latter book, which is the foundation of the ideology of the RSS, the BJP, and of Modi, Savarkar expounded his theory of territorial nationalism. Unless a people's beliefs, religion, and myths do not align with their territorial nationalism, their loyalty to the nation is suspect. Muslims and Christians, he declared, had other territorial loyalties, and were therefore not to be trusted. The loyalty of the Muslims, he writes, "must necessarily be divided between the land of their birth and the land of their Prophets . . . Mohammedans would naturally set the interests of their Holy land above those of their Motherland." Nationalism, which in India had a broadly ecumenical social sensibility, was reduced to religion—to the feeling of Hinduness, namely Hindutva. To be a nationalist was not to fight against British rule and to free India from imperialism. That kind of nationalism would welcome all those who fought against the British Raj—whether Dalits or Adivasis or Parsis or Bohras or Gorkhas or Nagas or Kashmiris or indeed Muslims of the Gangetic Plain or Hindus of the Deccan Plateau. That form of anti-colonial nationalism was anathema to Savarkar. It is that nationalism that sent him to prison in the Andaman Islands. His new nationalism was not against the British Raj. It was against his fellow Indians. Which is why the British allowed him to freely propagate his ideas—to hold *sabhas* and religious gatherings, to divide society for the benefit of the British rulers.

Well before he articulated his theory of Hinduness, Savarkar revealed his bigoted streak. At the age of twelve, he led a mob to vandalize a mosque.

There is a thick line that unites Savarkar to Modi. When he was released from prison, Savarkar met a disgruntled ex-Congressman, K.B. Hedgewar, who found in Savarkar his ideological anchor. A month after they met, in September 1925,

Hedgewar founded the RSS. This organization, with its long history of violence against Muslims, is Modi's home.

To preach hate—as the RSS does—is not enough to draw in sufficient numbers of people to one's side. Savarkar knew that people of good faith must be deceived in order to follow his movement He wrote his autobiography, *Life of Barrister Savarkar* (1926), under a false name—Chitragupta. It is an unabashed eulogy to Savarkar, with Savarkar as his own fanboy. The book is not easy to read because it glows so brightly for the subject, who is the author himself. Savarkar, Savarkar writes, "seemed to possess no few distinctive marks of character, such as an amazing presence of mind, indomitable courage, unconquerable confidence in his capability to achieve great things. Who could help admiring his courage and presence of mind?" (Ravindra Ramdas, the official publisher of Savarkar's book, revealed in the 1987 edition that Chitragupta was none other than Savarkar himself).

Courage? After he escaped conviction in the trial regarding the assassination of Gandhi, Savarkar once more begged the government to allow him to escape unscathed. "I shall refrain from taking part in any communal or political activity for any period the government may require in case I am released on that condition," he wrote. The author of Hindutva and the architect of the RSS drifted through history with this kind of cravenness.

RSS

The RSS is Modi's home. Savarkar is his ideological grandfather. But there are fathers closer yet—RSS leaders Hedgewar and M.S. Golwalkar. Under Modi's skin sits the scent of these men and their visions.

Hedgewar (1889-1940) was a young medic from Nagpur. We know little about his early years. As a Congress volunteer in 1920-21, he was arrested for a vitriolic speech on behalf of the *Khilafat* movement. But such wide nationalism would not appeal to him for long. He came under the wing of the radical Congress leader Dr. B.S. Moonje (1872-1948). Moonje is the link between European fascism and the RSS. On his way back to India after the Round Table Conference in London in 1931, Moonje stopped off in Italy. While in Rome from March 15 to 24, Moonje visited the Fascist Academy of Physical Education and the Opera Nazionale Balilla, the fascist youth organization. He was taken by the discipline and the fervor. Over two pages of his diary, Moonje writes of the Balilla's role in indoctrinating the youth of Italy into the fascist system. RSS drills—developed by Moonje—have their roots in the Balilla's weekly meetings, paramilitary trainings, and parades. Moonje delivered these elements of European fascism to the RSS through Hedgewar and Hedgewar's successor, M.S. Golwalkar (1906-1973). It was Golwalkar who would offer the most direct link between the ideology of European fascism and the RSS. In his book *We or Our Nationhood Defined* (1939), Golwalkar wrote:

> Come we next to the next ingredient of the Nation idea—Race, with which culture and language are inseparably connected, where religion is not the all-absorbing force that it should be. German Race pride has now become the topic of the day. To keep up the purity of the race and its culture, Germany shocked the world by her purging the country of the Semitic races—the Jews. Race pride at its highest has been manifested here. Germany has also shown how well-nigh impossible it is for races and cultures, having

differences going to the root, to be assimilated into one united
whole, a good lesson for us in Hindustan to learn and profit by.

This was written before the full evidence of the Final
Solution—the Holocaust—was clear. But, in the second edition
of the book from 1944 and in the third edition from 1945—long
after the full horror of the Nazi project was clear—Golwalkar
retained this paragraph.

What of fascism appealed to these men? The fascist obsession with social homogeneity and uniformity echoes through the
ideology of the RSS. Unlike the subcontinent's general tradition
of social inclusivity, the RSS drives a singular version of identity—
Hindutva. The RSS opposes any version of Hinduism that chal-
lenges the obsessive singularity of Hindutva.

Perhaps the RSS would not have been able to drive its ideology into the mainstream if the bourgeois parties—supposedly
secular—had not toyed with religious sentiment for political ends.
For instance, the Congress Party used religious division to weaken
the communist influence in the trade unions of Bombay, but it
was the authentic party of religious division—the Shiv Sena—that
earned the dividends. Or, the Congress would be afraid of con-
frontation against the RSS for fear of losing their hard-core Hindu
voters, such as when Chief Minister Govind Ballabh Pant refused
to arrest RSS functionaries—at the threshold of independence in
1947—who had been caught red-handed with a cache of inflam-
matory literature, maps, and weapons to use in sectarian riots in
Uttar Pradesh. Or, the Congress refused to displease the hard-core
Muslim clerics, such as when Prime Minister Rajiv Gandhi over-
turned the Supreme Court ruling to grant maintenance to Shah

Bano. Gandhi pushed through the Muslim Women (Protection on Divorce) Act of 1986 that delighted the mullahs and conservative Muslim men. These were diversionary tactics by the Congress Party to fool the electorate and to maintain power. But it was not the Congress that was able to control this dynamic. The RSS and the BJP rode the wave of offensiveness.

Indian society could not withstand the pressure. It cracked during the Ramjanmabhoomi movement in the 1980s and 1990s, when the RSS and the BJP conducted a nationwide campaign to destroy a sixteenth-century mosque in Ayodhya—the Babri Masjid—and build a temple to Ram on that very site. What began with stray protests increasingly amplified into violence, destruction, and even murder. The BJP and RSS, as a practice, always deny any link with violent incidents *ex post facto* and dismiss the miscreants as fringe elements. But the associations are stark, documented, palpable to all and sundry. And over the years the fringe elements have become mainstream and have gone on to hold important government offices. For example, current Chief Minister of Uttar Pradesh Yogi Adityanath was once seen as no more than a rabble-rousing priest. The hooligans of the past are now the rulers of the country.

Anything that does not mirror their vision of Indian society is to be silenced. The list is long and painful. The paintings of the artist M.F. Husain were torn, his exhibitions desecrated. Husain had to flee from his beloved homeland and die—heartbroken—in London. Cinema halls are attacked if certain films do not meet the RSS test (although movie moguls are astute—they pay the organizations or cut their own films to get past the RSS censors). This is not always possible. Sanjay Leela Bhansali made a film based on the fictional character Padmavati created by the medieval poet Malik Muhammad Jayasi in 1540. A fringe group, Karni Sena, took umbrage at the film, and its members manhandled Bhansali and his team on the film set. They warned him that they would burn every cinema hall that screens the film. Despite being approved by the Censor Board for Film Certification, BJP governments in the states banned the film. So it goes.

Academics and writers who cross the RSS and the BJP face the same kind of wrath. Because the Hindutva groups did not like James Laine's *Shivaji: Hindu King in Islamic India*, they vandalized the Bhandarkar Oriental Research Institute in Pune in 2004. A.K. Ramanujan's masterly essay *Three Hundred Ramayanas*—which documented the organic growth of a multi-narrative interpretation of the legend of Ram—was dropped from the English literature syllabus by the University of Delhi in 2012. Hindutva trolls attacked Audrey Truschke for her book *Aurangzeb*, while the Tamil writer Perumal Murugan was harassed for his fabulously inventive stories, and while the Adivasi writer Hansda Sowvendra lost his job for his book *The Adivasi Will Not Dance*.

Banning is one thing, murder another. The list here is long and painful. Australian Christian missionary Graham Staines and his two young sons were killed by the Bajrang Dal activist Dara Singh. Professor H.S. Sabharwal was beaten to death by activists from the BJP's student wing (ABVP), while rationalists and leftists Govind Pansare, Narendra Dabholkar, M.M. Kalburgi, and Gauri Lankesh were shot to death. Right-wing thugs did the killings, but there have been no arrests, no real investigation. This, of course, emboldens the right-wing thugs to pursue the underhanded work of their masters.

Matters are so ugly that in September 2017, NDTV anchor Ravish Kumar wrote an open letter to Modi, asking a provocative question. Troll armies on Twitter and WhatsApp—some followed by Modi's Twitter handle—had attacked Ravish Kumar. They called for his head. Ravish Kumar wrote, "I am making this letter public and sending it to you by post. If you know Nikhil Dadhich, Neeraj Dave and Akash Soni then please ask them that are they or their group planning to kill me?" Matters have reached such an awful place that a major television news anchor must ask such a question of the country's prime minister.

Savarkar, Hedgewar, Golwalkar—at one time marginal figures—are now in the mainstream. Three men who come from the RSS now hold the three highest positions in the Indian government—president (Ram Nath Kovind), vice president (Venkaiah Naidu), and prime minister (Narendra Modi).

Modi

Modi entered the world of the RSS when he was eight. His father came from a community that traditionally were pressers and sellers of vegetable oil. To support his family, the father ran a tea stall at the local railway station. Across the railway track was a Gujarati medium school where Modi went to school. His teachers remember him as an average student with a keen interest in theater and debate. Modi helped his father at the tea stall and spent his time at the RSS *shakha* (branch). It was the RSS shakha that took up most of Modi's time. In his formative years, Modi was being soaked with the ideals of Savarkar and Golwalkar.

At thirteen, Modi was married. When it came time to formally welcome his wife to his house, Modi abandoned everything and vanished for two years. There is no record of these years. When Modi returned home, he said he was wandering in the Himalayas in response to a "higher calling." The trope of abandonment of wife and children for a higher calling is deeply embedded in the Indian psyche. What may well be interpreted as the relinquishment of responsibility in other cultures could very well be a virtue in some circles.

The hero is always a gifted child, either misunderstood or a misfit. The calling comes at puberty, the rite of passage. The hero embarks on an adventure, a journey filled with insurmountable obstacles, hardship, even humiliation. Once he has made his conquest, the transformation happens. The hero, the individual, dies and what is reborn is the eternal man, the universal man whose solemn task and deed is to return to teach the world a lesson. The hero returns not merely to return, but to regenerate society, to transform it, to lead it into a social Nirvana.

After his return, Modi moved to Ahmedabad where he set up a tea stall near the RSS headquarters. In time, he moved into the RSS headquarters to work as the personal assistant to the chief. Modi entered the Gujarat RSS headquarters at a propitious time. The student agitation of 1974 and the National Emergency of 1975-76 provided the RSS with a new crop of activists, while the kings and princes—who lost their privy purses because Indira Gandhi snatched them away through a constitutional amendment in 1971—began to fund the RSS. This marginal group became socially acceptable. Modi's responsibilities increased: he was soon taking secretarial roles, opening and reading mail coming to the headquarters. Modi, seen as trustworthy, was sent to Nagpur—the RSS national headquarters—for a one-month officer training camp. He was then made the RSS in-charge for the RSS student front (ABVP) in Gujarat. He was a mentor to the students, like a "vein hidden under the skin." He was seen as too brash, as too public. But his work as an efficient organizer, getting RSS covert literature to its branches, saved him from repudiation.

When the Janata Party took power in 1977, many of Modi's senior colleagues became ministers and went to Delhi. Modi saw the opening. He returned to the Nagpur national headquarters for more advanced training and by 1981 was the main liaison between the RSS and all the front organizations in Gujarat. Modi was at the fulcrum of power.

Political power is elusive in the shadows. One needs to come to the surface to enjoy its benefits. Modi's transition out of the shadows began in 1987, when he was appointed to be the RSS organizational secretary for the Gujarat BJP. Communal friction sparked political gain for the BJP. More tension meant more insecurity meant greater numbers of people flocking to the behemoth for protection and for strength. The BJP organized a series of road shows to strike at the friction—the Nyay Yatra (1987), the Lok Shakti Rath Yatra (1989), and the Gujarat sector of the Ayodhya Rath Yatra (1991). Modi excelled as the organizer of these travelling theaters of hatred and insecurity. He was promoted to run the BJP President Murli Manohar Joshi's Ekta Yatra (1992) that ran from India's southern tip at Kanyakumari to Srinagar, the capital of Jammu and Kashmir. These road shows—and the blood left in their wake—raised the profile of the BJP, winning it, in Gujarat, 121 of 182 seats in 1995 (as opposed to eleven seats in 1985).

Power can do all kinds of things. It can create ambitions that are easily thwarted by internal rivalries. BJP leaders Shankarsinh

Vaghela and Keshubhai Patel first clashed, and then later Vaghela rebelled, and then Patel slipped. Modi was always in the shadows, whispering about their inadequacies and disloyalties. Patel became the chief minister in 1995, which sparked Vaghela's rebellion. The BJP high command sensed Modi's hand in these intrigues and shifted him to Delhi. It did not help. Modi had the pulse of his party. Vaghela formed a government in 1996 with Congress Party support, which allowed Modi to tell everyone in Delhi that he—Modi—was the first to sniff disloyalty in Vaghela. He would do the same to Patel after his government ran into problems with setbacks in local elections and two by-elections—an indictment of the inadequate relief work done in the aftermath of the 2001 Kutch earthquake. Modi whispered about Patel's failures, just as he had done about Vaghela.

Intrigue had always paid off for Modi. The campaign against Vaghela earned Modi the post of RSS organizational secretary in 1998. This allowed Modi to be the main liaison between the RSS and the BJP as well as the other Sangh Parivar organizations. Modi took to that job with gusto. He enjoyed the limelight, coming on television and offering his harsh views on world affairs. In a television debate about provocations from Pakistan, Modi said, "Chicken biryani nahi, bullet ka jawab bomb se diya jayega" (We won't give them chicken biryani, we will respond to a bullet with a bomb). This attitude of the hammer pleased the BJP base and the RSS brains. When Patel fell, Modi replaced him as chief minister of Gujarat.

Modi took charge of Gujarat in the immediate aftermath of 9/11 and the start of the War on Terror. Two months later, there was an attack on the Indian Parliament and a military buildup at the India-Pakistan border, with Gujarat as one of the flashpoints. Modi was prepared. He had his metaphoric bombs in hand. Older attitudes against Muslims—articulated by the founders of the RSS and cultivated by their followers—came to a head. They were sanctified by the United States, whose War on Terror had a decidedly anti-Muslim flavor. The Gujarat pogrom that followed the Godhra incident was part of this atmosphere. It is by now clear that the Gujarat government—with Modi at its head—was complicit in the riots. Inquiries that took place, which exonerated the government, were undermined by political pressure. These riots changed India's political landscape, as well as Modi's relationship to the Indian polity, forever. It was a watershed moment—and Modi understood that.

Modi never apologized for the pogrom. He remained unapologetic, even belligerent. This was something new. Politicians typically apologized for serious breaches, took some kind of responsibility and either resigned or were forgiven. Here was a leader with a massacre under his watch who remains brazen about it. Modi became a hero to the radical Right, the section that wanted this kind of bravura to be the mood of their leader. Modi cemented the loyalty of that growing section of the populace, and of the RSS and BJP cadre.

But he needed more to extend the reach of his power. He needed the backing of industrialists and financiers, of the big bourgeoisie. In 2003, the Confederation of Indian Industries (CII) hosted a special session between Modi and the top business elites. Adi Godrej (Godrej Industries) and Rahul Bajaj (Bajaj Industries) publicly censured Modi. Modi sat quietly, stewing, went to the podium and said, "Others have a vested interest in maligning Gujarat. What is your interest?" In a bout of Gujarati sub-nationalism, Modi surrounded himself with Gujarat's industrialists—Gautam Adani (Adani Group), Indravadan Modi (Cadila Pharmaceuticals), Karsan Patel (Nirma Group), and Anil Bakeri (Bakeri Engineers). They formed the Resurgent Group of Gujarat and publicly forced CII director-general Tarun Das to apologize and censure Godrej and Bajaj. Modi smirked in the wings. Modi came up for re-election in 2007. He wanted to cement the backing of the business elites. A glittering investment camp—Vibrant Gujarat Summit—became a campaign event for Modi. Ratan Tata (Tata Sons) endorsed him at this summit. It was enough. Modi won re-election. He morphed from the RSS man to a development-friendly business leader. The RSS man became the businessman's man.

More than anything Modi became Modi's man. He hastily isolated all his rivals—party elders were retired off to be part of the Margdarshak Mandal (Guiding Team), his peers were shifted away so Modi's henchmen could gather around, and his challengers felt the wrath of his diehard fans, the Bhakts and trolls who keep Modi's response after the Gujarat pogrom close to their hearts. The media owned by friendly corporate houses began to project Modi as a savior, as a larger than life figure. It was no surprise when Modi declared that he had a fifty-six-inch chest—the scale of his ambitions could not be contained in anything less than that. Modi's closest ally, Amit Shah, helped run the ground game, which included making the role of Muslims in elections marginal (this was the actual *Gujarat Model*, which was exported to the rest of the country after 2014). Between seduction and intimidation, Modi coasted to the prime ministership in 2014. His party won less than a third of the votes, and benefitted from the first past the post system. You wouldn't know that. The celebrations suggested that Modi had won in a landslide. How could this behemoth, this savior, win anything less than the hearts of all Indians?

Modi's Political Grammar

An old Persian fable—"The Devil's Syrup"—highlights the purpose of the Devil: to disrupt, create chaos, and gain power through anarchy. An honest man enters a confectioner's shop. The Devil quietly drips a bit of sugar syrup on the confectioner's balding head. A fly sits on his head and begins to suck the syrup. The honest man sees the fly, takes off his shoe and whacks the fly on the confectioner's head. The confectioner is angry. He doesn't believe that the honest man was merely hitting the fly. The honest man says that was the only reason, but the confectioner does not believe him. A fight ensues. Others arrive. The shop is destroyed.

"The Devil's Syrup" is a story about the universality of deception. The syrup of propaganda produces disaffection, which erupts in an alternative narrative, points to enemies, disorients people, and delivers power to the deceivers. Truth is suppressed, incomplete information is provided, and lies are dressed up to look like "facts." An emotional not a rational response is evoked by the deceiver.

Deception is one part of the grammar of Modi's politics. Another is the production of division and of fear. These are the pieces of Modi's strategy, what has enabled Modi to come to power.

There is a classic tale of the Umayad Caliph Muawiya who wanted to discredit the house of Abdul Muttalib, Muhammad's patriarch. He asked his counsel Amr bin al-Aas to find a man from the house of Abdul Muttalib who had a character flaw. Amr recommended Aqeel bin Abi Talib, Muhammad's cousin. When Aqeel visits Muawiya's court, the Caliph had the Surah al-Masad (from the Quran) recited in the court:

> May the hands of Abu Lahab be ruined, and ruined is he. His wealth will not avail him or that which he gained. He will [enter to] burn in a Fire of [blazing] flame and his wife [as well]—the carrier of firewood. Around her neck is a rope of [twisted] fibre.

Then Muawiya mocks Aqeel by saying, "Don't you know Aqeel that the Abu Lahab mentioned in these verses is your paternal uncle?" Aqeel immediately quips, "Why don't you disclose that the carrier of firewood, the woman mentioned in these verses is your paternal aunt?"

This whole display of dialogue between Muawiya and Aqeel is farcical. The idea is not to invoke an ethical debate but to suppress information, present it as banter, create an emotional upheaval through humiliation, and win legitimacy by creating a false sense of victory.

William Gibson, the science fiction writer, says perceptively, "Fascism first causes, then thrives on the chaos for which it presents itself as the sole cure."

Modi arrives in the cow belt in Bihar during the election campaign of 2014. He invokes the "pink revolution" that will overtake the country. India, Modi says, is the largest meat exporter and he accuses meat exporters of colluding with the butchers—who are mainly Muslims. Modi didn't say that one of the largest meat exporters is an active member of the BJP and that the other largest meat exporter is a very loud public supporter of the BJP. All the classic tropes are at play. A farcical premise is set up, a debate ensues to distract the public, information is suppressed, an element of fear is introduced, and the only savior is the perpetrator of this fear. And then there is the chilling dynamic that gets set up—six months after this speech, a man was falsely accused of storing beef in his house, then he was lynched and murdered in broad daylight.

To gaslight is a devious project—to make someone doubt what they know, play with their memory, make them feel like what they are being accused of is what they have done. The forces of Hindutva have made gaslighting part of their arsenal over the past several decades.

In the first year of independence, Rajendra Prasad—India's first president—who sympathized with the right wing and even with Hindutva, wrote (on March 14, 1948) to India's Home Minister Sardar Patel, who also sympathized with these forces:

> I am told that RSS people have a plan of creating trouble. They have got a number of men dressed as Muslims and looking like Muslims who are to create trouble with the Hindus by attacking them and thus inciting the Hindus. Similarly there will be some Hindus among them who will attack Muslims and thus incite Muslims. The result of this kind of trouble amongst the Hindus and Muslims will be to create a conflagration.

The idea is to create suspicion, doubt, and a particular perception that establishes a stereotypical image of the other. Manufacture the image if need be even through unethical and illegitimate means because the end justifies the process. Once the stereotype is established, once people's beliefs are firmed up then no amount of refusal, rebuttal, or corroboration by facts will matter. The narrative necessarily would transform into one of pride and feelings, glory and humiliation, and all one would care is to restore the same. The WhatsApp messages, fake news websites, tilted debates by biased news anchors, and visual depictions of a particular narrative in advertisements and billboards, serve the same purpose of stoking the manufactured perception. Once the divisiveness cleaves through the society then even genocide and homicide become legitimate. Ultimately, the ethnic cleansing will ensure a pure race, an unsullied culture, a golden age, and an Elysium where everything will be in harmony. The enemy with its filth—culture, language, stories, cuisine, symbols, and architecture—would have been flushed away.

In the epic tale of *Tilism-e-Hoshruba*, Amir Hamza, the lord of conjunction, is fighting the false god Laqa. When besieged, Laqa makes one of his followers, King Suleiman Amber-Hair, write a letter to Suleiman's neighboring kingdoms,

> Lord Laqa has sought refuge with me after suffering reverses at the hands of Hamza. You must needs rush to his aid, not out of any consideration for me but because he is your God. You must kill his foes and restore him to his divine throne. If you make delay after reading these words, the wrath of His Lordship will wipe you out of existence. His Lordship Laqa indulges these creatures who persecute him only out of mercy. He desists from killing them and maintains that these creatures were made in the reveries of his drunken sleep. As he was oblivious of himself in the ecstasies of his

inebriation, his pen of destiny wrote them down as rebellious and vain. Now that destiny cannot be altered. It is for this reason that our Lord is unable to efface their existence and is so wroth with them that when these creatures beseech him with their contrite pleas, he scorns them and flies away from them. Seeing no hope of their redemption in Lord Laqa, these creatures have vowed whole-sale rebellion against him. It is therefore incumbent upon you to arrive here post-haste to assist our Lord.

Either you are with Lord Laqa or you are against him. This is George W. Bush's logic after 9/11—either you are with us or you are against us. It is Modi's choice now, either you are with him or against him. If you do not stand with Lord Laqa or Bush or Modi, then the world will fall on your head. You are compelled to stand with the Lord, with Bush, with Modi. Modi's trolls twist every debate into a binary—either support Modi and display one's patriotism or be an anti-national and be seen as seditious. Modi is India, India is Modi. The enemy is the enemy: it must be defeated and Modi must be applauded.

Farce

Modi is the savior. He is silent. He does not denounce. He does not step into the fray.

The landscape of India is littered with horrendous lynching events, killings by "fringe" supporters of the Sangh Parivar. Littered with nonsense blabberings of Modi's cabinet ministers and party members. Littered with threats against writers and actors. Modi says nothing. He remains silent. This litter is not to be cleaned up by his Swachh Bharat Abhiyan (Clean India Mission).

Junaid Khan was lynched on a train for allegedly carrying beef. Protests took place across India—#NotInMyName. Modi issued a statement, "No one spoke about protecting cows more than Mahatma Gandhi and Acharya Vinoba Bhave. Yes. It should be done. But, killing people in the name of Gau Bhakti is not acceptable. This is not something Mahatma Gandhi would approve." That is it. Cows should be protected. Gandhi would not approve of the killing of Junaid. But does Modi approve?

When dominant caste vigilantes mercilessly flogged Dalits for transporting dead cows in Gujarat, Modi offered his enigmatic views. He said that miscreants who bring disrepute to society commit seventy to eighty percent of the acts of violence. Does that mean that twenty to thirty percent of the acts of violence committed by the vigilantes are acceptable?

When asked about the victims of the Gujarat pogrom, Modi said that when one is riding in the backseat of a car and if the car hits a puppy, the passenger feels bad about it. The pogrom becomes an accident, the victim is a stray animal and Modi is the bystander.

India trundles towards the land of farce. The signs are visible now. A man in Meerut said that he would build a temple for his god—Modi—with a hundred-foot statue of his idol. This is not the first temple to Modi. That was built in Gujarat in 2014. Modi disapproved of it at that time. Now he is silent. The first time it was an embarrassment; the second time it is a farce.

Grabbing hold of this farce, this distraction, is the insidiousness of the RSS. It wishes to change the Constitution of India and to alter the fundamental social fabric of the land. Plutarch writes of a ship whose parts are all altered. If the ship is no longer made of its original parts, is it the same ship? Is India fated to be like Plutarch's Ship of Theseus? What will the apologists of Modi say when they wake one day and find that the republic that they lived in is no longer recognizable?

In this new land, Modi will be its principal deity. In his *The Hero with a Thousand Faces*, Joseph Campbell describes the vanity of the tyrant,

> The inflated ego of a tyrant is a curse to himself and his world—no matter how his affairs may seem to prosper. Self-terrorized, fear-haunted, alert at every hand to meet and battle back the antici-pated aggressions of his environment, which are primarily the reflections of the uncontrollable impulses to acquisition within himself, the giant of self-achieved independence is the world's messenger of disaster, even though, in his mind, he may entertain himself with humane intentions.

Somewhere, Ghalib is singing his old poem,

hastī ke mat fareb meñ aa jā.iyo 'asad'
aalam tamām halqa-e-dām-e-ḳhayāl hai

Be not beguiled by this ego, O Asad!
This universe is but a realm of imagination.

ERDOĞAN
A Normal Man

Burhan Sönmez

Victim

WHEN ERDOĞAN STARTED to run for office in 1994, he took his wedding ring from his finger. He held it up to the people during a speech. "That is my only wealth," he said in front of the press. Five years later, in 1999, he stated, "If some day you hear that Tayyip Erdoğan has become so rich you should consider that he has committed sinful things."

This was the year when he ascended to the peak of his fame as a *victim*. Erdoğan was convicted by the Turkish state for reciting a poem during a rally. The poem, written by Turkish nationalist Ziya Gökalp a century before, was said to be changed from its original by Erdoğan; he added in some extra elements.

> The mosques are our barracks
> The domes our helmets
> The minarets our bayonets
> And the believers our soldiers.

At that time, Erdoğan was the mayor of Istanbul. Reciting the poem got the attention of the secular-sensitive judiciary. Having been sentenced to ten months in prison, Erdoğan served four months in jail. The prison was not a prison. It was a prison in name only. They had converted it into an office for him. He had a secretary in the prison with him. The secretary's name is Hasan Yeşildağ, who deliberately committed a small crime in order to get into prison and welcome Erdoğan. They prepared a special ward for Erdoğan. It had a television, a fridge, and a sofa. Visitors came daily to see him. National and international luminaries came to see him. Their interest suggested that they saw him as a figure of political promise for Turkey.

When Erdoğan left prison, he did not wait long to depart from his political party, which was saturated in traditional Islamist discourse. Erdoğan had learned a lesson. Not to abandon Islamism, but to walk away from its traditional—and marginal—form. He said he had changed, but he never pointed out what parts of his ideology had changed.

These were the years of turmoil for the Turkish economy and for Turkish politics. Erdoğan met with international celebrities, such as George Soros, and with elected officials from the United States. He was seen as a moderate Muslim leader who could provide a positive example for the Middle East.

◆

In 2002, Erdoğan's newly-formed political party—Justice and Development Party (AKP)—won a surprising victory in the elections. It won thirty-four percent of the vote and—because of the system of Turkish politics—sixty-six percent of the seats in the parliament. Erdoğan had the complete support of almost all Western governments and the European Union. He was seen as a symbol of change and moderation as well as a bridge between cultures—the cultures of the West and Islam. When the Constitutional Court investigated the AKP in 2008 on the allegation that it had breached the secular basis of the Turkish Republic, none other than Queen Elizabeth II of Great Britain paid an unexpected visit to Turkey. She was a guest of Turkish President Abdullah Gül—Erdoğan's man. The visit was interpreted as support of the West for Erdoğan and his government. Two months after Queen Elizabeth's visit, the Constitutional Court rejected the proposal to close the AKP. The vote in the Court was close—six judges won over five. Four of the five judges who voted to close down the AKP said that the party was at "the centre of anti-secular activities." It was of no consequence. Erdoğan got away with it, backed by the West.

Erdoğan sees himself as the victim. He has pushed for and supported the fabricated and politically motivated cases against journalists, army officers, and dissident politicians over the past few years. But their problems are not his. "Where were you when I was sent to jail?" he responds plaintively when he is asked about the detention of the dissidents. Everyone can be victimized, but Erdoğan is the one and only *real victim*. It first appeared that he was playing a political game. But now it seems that this is Erdoğan's genuine sensibility. He truly thinks of himself as the victim. Erdoğan The Victim.

Erdoğan does not care about those who are not on his side. In 2011, he visited a small town in north-eastern Turkey. The locals protested the government's anti-environmental policy, which had terrible effects in the region. The police acted with violence against the protestors. A school teacher was killed. Erdoğan was asked about this during a live television program. He neither showed remorse nor expressed any sadness about the death of the school teacher. No one could be named a victim while Erdoğan himself was a victim.

After nearly two decades, Erdoğan read the same poem again that was the reason for his imprisonment. This time no official body opposed him. Official bodies—such as the police, army, judiciary, universities, and media—are now on his side. There is no one left to defy him.

This is a snapshot of where our story begins and where it has now ended.

Innocent

The Turkish Constitution says that a candidate for the presidency must have graduated from an institution of higher education. This means that the president has to have been at university for four years.

Erdoğan graduated from Aksaray High School of Commerce in 1981. That was a two-year school at that time. When he was prime minister and when he prepared to run for the presidency, Erdoğan claimed that his former high school had merged with the University of Marmara and that it had been converted into a four-year school in his last year. It was all a bit confusing. The University of Marmara was founded in 1982. Erdoğan's school joined it in 1983. Erdoğan graduated in 1981.

Journalists as well as parliamentarians questioned Erdoğan's version of events. They looked at the documents that he had produced. There was something wrong with the documents. The documents from the 1980s used two fonts—Calibri and Malgrin Gothic. But Calibri was only introduced in 2005, while Malgrin Gothic came on the market in 2008 from Microsoft.

Erdoğan loves to talk about himself and about his past. His stories suggest that he is the chosen one. He has so many memories of his life, including of his time as a student—except for his period at university. Some journalists asked those who studied with Erdoğan to come forward and tell their stories, or just to provide pictures of their time at school. No one dared to speak up. At the last minute, the University of Marmara claimed that Erdoğan was their student—even though it was founded two years after Erdoğan graduated from his school.

Erdoğan ran for the presidency and he won the election. No one could legally challenge his claim that he has a four-year college degree. Erdoğan does not like to be questioned about this matter. He is happy to send all his rivals to prison. But the "fake diploma" is the only subject that one can raise without being sent to prison. If he goes after the accuser in a court, then he will have to prove—formally—to the court that his university diploma is genuine. Erdoğan is stuck in a cul-de-sac. Although this has not hurt him at all.

Erdoğan now has de facto immunity; his heavy hands are capable of squashing anyone. The institutions of the law are not able to question him or his relatives. When his son was accused of money laundering a few years ago, all the officers who dared to file the dossier were removed from their posts. When his son-in-law's emails were leaked by hackers last year and published, the Turkish journalists who used those documents were arrested. There is no room to mention his other activities—manipulation and theft during the time of elections or sending his most effective opponent—Kurdish leader Selahattin Demirtaş—to prison. Demirtaş wrote a poem—"Contagious Bravery"—while behind bars. It could not be published. A prosecutor forbade it. Erdoğan calls Demirtaş a zealot while reminding his audience of his own imprisonment for reciting a poem. Erdoğan is the only victim; he does not want to share the pleasure of being a victim with anyone else.

Erdoğan's mind works in two parts, with two different mechanisms. He has recently stated that those who go abroad to study return home as the agent of foreign forces. "They become voluntary agents and dedicated disciples of the West," he said. But Erdoğan's four children studied abroad. His two daughters went to Indiana University, while his sons went to Harvard University and the London School of Economics.

A victim is always innocent. He never makes a mistake. If there is a mistake, then someone else is to blame. Not the eternal victim. Erdoğan was once the best friend of Bashar al-Assad of Syria. Their families spent time with each other. When the alliance of the United States and the Saudis began their assault on Syria, Erdoğan took part in it. He blamed Assad at a personal level. "He lied to me, he deceived me," he said. This rhetoric of personal betrayal is now commonplace. Erdoğan used it to describe the oscillating relationship he has had with Germany's Angela Merkel and Barack Obama of the United States.

The most significant *deception* has not been by a foreign leader, however, but by a formerly close domestic ally—the Gülen movement led by Fethullah Gülen. Gülen and his movement were Erdoğan's best allies for two decades. This is the largest Islamist movement in Turkey and in the Turkish diaspora. Gülen comes from a right-wing background. He supported the military coup in 1980 and enjoys close relations with the United States, where he now lives. It would not be an exaggeration to say that Gülen has been the most influential political figure in Turkey in the twenty-first century. With a long view and a powerful organizational structure, Gülen has been able to occupy all the main institutions of the country—including the universities, the police force, the military, and the judiciary. His followers could be seen in parliament, in the embassies, and in the media.

It was Gülen who persuaded Erdoğan to depart from the traditional Islamist political party and ideology and to found a new political party—namely the AKP. It was Gülen who introduced Erdoğan to the Western world, including leaders of the United States. It was Gülen who packaged Erdoğan as the promise of change and reform in the region. Erdoğan, the good student, began to use the language of liberalism—speaking about democracy, tolerance as well as justice, including language about class relations and LGBT rights.

In the second decade of their "sacred" alliance, Erdoğan and Gülen apparently felt that the time had come to occupy everything—to put their hand on every institution in Turkey. But the real question was—whose hand would be on top? Tensions rose in the alliance, and then the rift opened up.

In December 2013, the police and prosecution services published information about how some politicians and businessmen had been involved with bribery and corruption. Around the same time, the recordings of conversations with these people were leaked on social media platforms. Four ministers in Erdoğan's cabinet were implicated. There were also recordings of conversations between Erdoğan and his son about money laundering. It was seen—immediately—as a salvo in a war between Erdoğan and the Gülen movement, the latter having its tentacles in the police, in the office of the prosecutors, and in the judiciary. Erdoğan reacted fiercely. He fired police officers, prosecutors, and judges involved in the case. He had to sacrifice the four ministers in his cabinet who were caught on tape.

Erdoğan and his son came out unscathed. So did two other crucial figures. Reza Zarrab, an Iranian businessman, had been at the center of the operation of bribery and corruption. He was accused of illegal gold trafficking between Iran and Turkey. He had been arrested, but then—at Erdoğan's orders—was released. The police found millions of dollars hidden in a shoebox in the apartment of the director of Halkbank, Süleyman Aslan. He was arrested. Erdoğan had him released. He stopped all legal processes by appointing friendly police officers and judges.

The tussle between Erdoğan and Gülen did not end easily. In 2016, Gülen's men took a final step. They attempted a military coup, which was unsuccessful. Since Erdoğan got information of the plot beforehand, he let it take place. When the coup failed—largely because the authorities knew it was going to happen—Erdoğan used it to strike out against the Gülen movement. He spoke to the press, while hundreds of people were being killed on the streets, and said: *This move is a great gift from God to us.* Erdoğan took advantage of this "gift" and began to smash his rivals by declaring a state of emergency. The government suspended the European Convention on Human Rights (ECHR) and extended the detention period for those arrested to thirty days from two days. The entire state structure shuddered as Erdoğan's government fired 150,000 public service workers—including 5,800 academics and fifty-one thousand school teachers. The purge did not spare the army or the police. It ran through every institution of the state. Apart from being the biggest jailer of journalists (170 in prison at last count), the government now went after lawyers (one thousand in prison). About eighty mayors went to prison along with a dozen parliamentarians—all of whom from the pro-Kurdish People's Democratic Party (HDP), the party of Demirtaş who wrote his poem in prison.

Turkey now struggles to survive the war between these two Islamist powers. When the forces of Erdoğan and Gülen began to fight each other, the left-wing organizations and the Kurdish opposition were the ones who were targeted. Most of the academics and school teachers who were dismissed and most of the media outlets that have been shut down belong to the progressive movement. Since the "failed coup" of 2016, the country has been in a permanent state of emergency. Parliament has been bypassed. It has become a mere template with no real role in the making of policy. Erdoğan rules from his newly built White Palace. His palace has sealed off the Turkish parliament. What Erdoğan has done was Gülen's dream. It is now Erdoğan's reality. It is the kind of dream that has thrown the whole nation into a nightmare.

The last time that we saw the great alliance between Erdoğan and Gülen was during the Gezi Park uprising in May 2013. Millions of people took to the streets for two weeks to resist Erdoğan's plan to turn the tiny Gezi Park in the heart of Istanbul into a shopping mall. The resistance around Gezi amplified the voice of people who had been silenced under the long shadow of religious power. Erdoğan, like all autocratic leaders, used two tools: violence and deceit. He refused the claim that he planned to build a shopping mall in the park at the same time as he sent in the police—manned by Gülen supporters—to break up the protestors. The result was that the authorities arrested five thousand people, wounded four thousand people and killed eight young people. Gezi Park was saved.

When the police were criticized for using excessive force, Erdoğan appeared on the stage and used his usual language of mercilessness. "They ask about who gave the order to the police. Me. I gave the order," he said. He accused the protestors of hurting the economy. It was their protest, he said, that raised the value of the US dollar from 1.8 to 1.9 Turkish lira. He called the protestors enemies of the state.

Things are worse now. It costs four Turkish lira to buy a dollar. Erdoğan accuses others for this. Nothing is his responsibility. His policies are innocent. He is innocent.

Normal

Having returned from abroad after some years I went in a smartphone shop in Turkey as I wanted to buy a charger for my cell phone. The seller offered me an expensive one and said, "This is original."

"But it is expensive," I said.

"Then, I have that one, five times cheaper," he said.

"Okay, if this is original, what is that one?" I asked.

"It is the normal one," said the shopkeeper.

Such phones would have been called "imitation" or "artificial" phones. But that's in the past. Now they are "normal." Our language shows us how much has changed in our politics and in our culture. Since the original and true things are lost, anything fake and artificial can replace it and become "normal."

In this new century, Erdoğan stands for normality. His reign has already lasted longer than that of Mustafa Kemal Atatürk, who founded and ruled the modern Turkish Republic for fifteen years from 1923 to 1938. Erdoğan counts the years when he compares himself with Atatürk. He believes that the destruction of the Ottoman Empire—carried out by Atatürk and his comrades a century ago—was a mistake. Erdoğan has given himself the historic task of reversing Atatürk's work and reviving the empire. That is what he believes and that is what his followers desire. They see Erdoğan as the chosen one for the nation not only of the Turks, but also for Muslims.

Erdoğan's prominent supporters define the modern Turkish Republic as a "bracket" between the Ottoman Empire and another kind of empire. This "bracket," they believe, opens up a mysterious sentence; it is now time to close that sentence. Erdoğan says that to end that period of history, the period between the "brackets," there is no need to respect the law. "Two drunkards" made that law, he says. It is not difficult to understand what he means by this phrase. The "two drunkards" he refers to are Atatürk and his friend İsmet İnönü, who became president after Atatürk's death.

They are well known for their love of *raki*, that milky alcohol of the Turkish people.

Drinkers apparently obsess Erdoğan. In 1989, he ran for the mayorship of Beyoğlu District in Istanbul, but lost. He objected to the outcome of the election and took the case to the court. When the judge appeared to go against him, Erdoğan called him a "drunkard." He was detained for a week and made to pay a fine.

Erdoğan's conservative political worldview is one thing, but his temper is another. It is not easy to manage. There are rumors that he slapped some cabinet ministers. That he has attacked ordinary citizens is no rumor. In 2014, Turkey experienced a mining disaster when 301 miners died underground. It is said to be the biggest mining accident in the world. The accident came due to poor working conditions. There was no administrative surveillance of conditions in the mine. A few days after the incident, Erdoğan visited the small town where the miners' families lived. A protest greeted him, with angry slogans filling the air. At one point, Erdoğan had to take refuge in a shop inside the market. There, Erdoğan grabbed a protester and began to hit him, while calling out, "You are the Jew's semen." Someone in the shop filmed this attack. It appeared on social media platforms. Before long the film disappeared, like so many other things. It vanished. Erdoğan's cyber-farm did its work well. The farm's workers erase and destroy anything on the Internet that is against Erdoğan. Even some of Erdoğan's speeches are inaccessible. Erdoğan's conversations with his son about hiding money—and many other recordings—have disappeared. Thousands of websites, including Wikipedia, are forbidden inside Turkey. Twitter and Facebook

ERDOĞAN: A NORMAL MAN

are shut down whenever the government thinks they are too aggressive against Erdoğan. This is Turkey's *normal.*

Erdoğan began his life as a conservative Islamist. Then he changed his status to being a moderate Islamist. Now he is on the march to becoming a new kind of *sultan.* It has been a long march—taking charge of the traditional authoritarian systems in society and in the state as well as creating new kinds of institutions in both state and society to consolidate his power.

In the 1970s, Erdoğan got involved with the youth division of the Islamist MSP—the National Salvation Party. The military coup of 1980 changed the political field in Turkey. The coup leaders arrested 650,000 people, closed down parliament, shut down trade unions, and shuttered publishing houses. Political parties—including those of the right and of the religious variety—were closed down. The coup was a right-wing coup, but it could not tolerate right-wing parties. It was a total suffocation of Turkish society. This was at the height of the Cold War. In the Middle East and South Asia, the United States was playing with a policy of the Green Belt—the support of Islamist elements, however extreme, to quell communist influence. Erdoğan's political framework developed in this period. His *normal* is the normal of an alliance between the imperialist West and the Islamist East.

It was no surprise when Erdoğan, in 2015, chose İsmail Kahraman to be the spokesperson of the Turkish Parliament. Kahraman comes to the AKP from the extreme right. His youth was spent in battle against the anti-imperialist youth who wanted to stop the visit of US warships to Istanbul in the 1960s.

The army smashed the progressive reservoirs of Turkish society and politics. The attack on the left was even sharper after the collapse of the Soviet Union. Islamism, long cultivated by the army and the United States, rose in Turkish politics. In 1994, a marginal politician such as Erdoğan managed to become the mayor of Istanbul, the biggest city in the country. His language resonated with anti-secularism ("A man cannot be both a Muslim and secular at the same time") and with misogyny ("Men and women cannot be equal. This is against their nature") and with ruling-class ideology ("We use the state of emergency for the benefit of our business world. When there is a possibility of a workers' strike we immediately stop it by using the state of emergency").

They call this the state of *precious loneliness*. It has become Turkey's destiny, they say. The Western world, they say, is jealous of Erdoğan as a world-historical leader. The West wants to block the dawn of the Turkish and Muslim nation, which is the bright star of mankind.

Erdoğan and his people in the media use the language of loneliness, of precious loneliness. Anyone who is against Erdoğan is said to be against the nation. This is the cliché of populism— still finding buyers everywhere, from the United States to the Philippines.

At a certain point, the fake becomes normal and insanity turns into normality.

Lucky

Ahmet Şık, an investigative journalist, was preparing a book about the secret organization of the Gülen movement in the official institutions. While he was in the process of writing his book, the police arrested him and confiscated his manuscript, titled *The Imam's Army*. This was in March 2011. The arrest appeared to be an operation to save the Gülen movement. Erdoğan was on the stage again. This was six years before his rift with Gülen. "There are some books that are more effective than bombs," he said in support of the imprisonment of Şık.

After the "failed coup" in 2016, there was a funeral for the victims of the coup at a mosque. Erdoğan was present. An imam gave a sermon that condemned educated people instead of the coup plotters. "O mighty god," he said, "protect us from the evil of educated people." This was not a sentence pronounced accidentally. When a pro-Erdoğan academic said, "The most traitors are found among well-educated people" on a television show, it was seen as utterly normal. No one objected. What is there to object to when this is a normal statement?

Left-wing groups and parties, trade unions, students, journalists, writers, intellectuals of different forms—these have been the most determined in the opposition against Erdoğan. In the lead is the Kurdish resistance. This unity is the base for a democratic opening in Turkey. If they have been unsuccessful thus far, it is because they have never united against Erdoğan's government. They are divided for different reasons. Their division gives Erdoğan a great advantage.

Erdoğan has built himself a White Palace. It has a thousand rooms. The White Palace has been at the center of a set of debates—it is not only seen as a white elephant, but it was also built illegally on public fields. Erdoğan's regime did not bother to ask for permission from any government office, nor did it bother to apply for an official permit for the construction of this palace in the heart of Ankara, the capital city of Turkey. If Erdoğan is normal, then his practice is normal too—if he is the norm, then his building is the norm as well. No inspector or judge will question the lack of permits, just as no one questions his wealth. His wedding ring was his only asset. Now he is among the richest statesmen in the world. His wealth, he said in 2014, is in the multiple millions of dollars. It was the same year that uncomfortable videos of Erdoğan began to disappear from the Internet including the video in which he said, "If some day you hear that Tayyip Erdoğan has become so rich, then you should consider that he has committed sinful things."

"Erdoğan" is now a familiar name in such leaked documents as those revealed by WikiLeaks and by the *Süddeutsche Zeitung* (the Panama Papers). When a journalist asked Erdoğan how his son managed to buy a ship, he responded, "A ship and a shipish [a smaller ship] are different things." His personal wealth has swollen upwards while the national economy has withered. Turkey's external debt has reached $432 billion (2017). Fifteen years ago, when the AKP came to power, the external debt was $129 billion.

That is the picture of a country where some men have been *lucky*, while the majority have been slipping downhill. Erdoğan is a *lucky* man.

PUTIN
So Sexy It Hurts

Lara Vapnyar

So sexy it hurts.

I HATE TO admit it, but every time I see yet another topless photo of Putin, Right Said Fred's song starts playing in my head.

Too sexy for my shirt

So sexy it hurts.

This doesn't happen by accident or as a result of the dark workings of my perverse mind. This happens because I'm a victim of the Russian propaganda machine. Putin's "sexiness" and the idea of his "sexual prowess" has been carefully cultivated as part of his overall political image.

I'm not sure whose idea it was and when exactly the great work on Putin's sexiness started, but he hadn't always been "too sexy for his shirt," certainly not as a younger man.

Putin in the 1980s, 1990s, and early 2000s was the opposite of sexy. A modest KGB officer working on the sidelines who grew to be a quiet bureaucrat and evolved into a tough but self-effacing ruler, a man without qualities, an invisible man, "a man without a face," as Masha Gessen calls him in her seminal biography.

The first and rather shocking awareness of Putin's sexiness came to people a few years before the election of 2012, after a series of photos depicting him in the midst of bold and striking adventures appeared in the press.

There was Putin in 2009, vacationing in Siberia. Climbing trees. Having simple meals with villagers. Swimming in freezing Siberian rivers. Diving in the world's deepest lake, Baikal. Riding horses down the rugged terrain while shirtless.

The UK's *Daily Mail* noted that: "Tony Blair may prefer ritzy yachts in the Caribbean, but it's a hardman's life for Vladimir Putin," leaving no doubt about which man that venerable publication preferred.

Then there was Putin in 2010 hunting a whale off the coast of Kamchatka Peninsula. Choppy waters, steel-gray sky, Putin dressed in macho red and black colors leaning over the edge of a rubber boat, aiming his dart gun with great concentration. He did manage to kill a whale (or rather, his team managed to create the impression that he had). The mission was a great success.

The Guardian reported that "when the boat skidded onto the beach, Putin hopped off and made a beeline for waiting reporters. Clearly in his element, Putin replied jovially to a question as to whether the endeavour was dangerous. 'Living in general is dangerous,' he quipped. Asked why he got involved, he replied, 'Because I like it. I love the nature.'" At least he didn't say "I am nature" like Jackson Pollock once did.

Then there was Putin entering the cage of a lively leopard, tracking a Siberian tiger, putting a collar on a huge polar bear (the animal was heavily sedated, but still). Yet nothing could quite compare with his highly publicized flying with cranes stunt. This was taking publicity to another level.

The idea was for Putin to board the motorized hang glider, get up in the air, and lead the flock of real live cranes toward their migration destination, acting like a leader of the flock or, in other words, an alpha male. All of the participating humans did their job really well. With the help of the experienced pilot, Putin did get up in the air and flew in the needed direction. The only problem was with the cranes—apparently the birds were too confused to form the proper geometric shape and follow their human leader. But then who cares about the birds? The majority of the Russian population certainly didn't.

The Western press as well as the Russian intellectual elite pronounced the stunt a laughable failure, a desperate vanity project of an unstable aging man. But Putin has always cared very little about the Western press, and possibly even less about the Russian intellectual elite. The only thing that mattered was the opinion of the general Russian population. And the population loved it. They saw their leader soar into the sky on a heroic quest. They saw their leader as a bold and sexy alpha male. Bolder, sexier, more alpha than any other world leader. That was the idea that stayed in people's minds. And the birds that didn't make it were instantly and easily forgotten.

But if the cranes stunt was merely suggestive of Putin's sexual prowess, there were other, more transparent publicity tricks. The most amazing of them was the series of videos credited to an advertising agency Aldus ADV.

In one of them, a young Russian woman asks a fortune-teller about her intended. "It's my first time," she confides, "I want it to be for love." Everything in the scene, from the woman's words to her nervousness suggests that she's about to lose her virginity. The fortune-teller pulls a card, and guess who is on it? You're absolutely right, Vladimir Putin! Because who else would be better at taking your virginity with love?

Another video of the series shows a young woman in a doctor's office. Her concern is the same. She wants her first time to happen just right. The doctor talks to her about the importance of protection. Safety is important, especially during the first time (I'd say it's equally important during subsequent attempts, but let's stay on topic). And just then the camera shifts to the calendar on the wall. Now, guess who is on that calendar? You're right again, Vladimir Putin! Because who else is responsible enough to ensure the needed level of protection during your first time? After that we follow the young woman to the polls. She looks enthusiastic, and we're confident that she'll make the "right" choice.

The Aldus ADV agency said to the press that it created the clips with the aim of targeting younger voters and making them excited about taking part in the elections. But I think they also targeted a much larger demographic by planting the idea of Putin as a strong and capable lover.

Soon after the election of 2012, the media was flooded with the new wave of images speaking of Putin's sexual prowess. This time the rumors were focused on Putin's alleged lover, former gymnastics champion Alina Kabaeva, then thirty-years old. People were saying that the couple had maintained a relationship for years and even had a child together. Putin himself denied the rumor, and there is no way to know whether this was a fact or a lie, accidentally spilled dirt or a carefully leaked open secret. But regardless of the true state of events, it's hard to think of a more perfect woman to fit the role of Putin's public mistress. Kabaeva is not just a younger woman. She is an extraordinarily robust and proficient younger woman. One can hardly imagine her submitting to a lesser lover, or one incapable of killing a whale or handling a polar bear.

Around the same time, Putin announced that he was divorcing his wife of almost thirty years. Lyudmila Putina had always been a kind of "silent partner" in the marriage, and the divorce was as quiet and amicable as they come. In a carefully staged televised announcement, Putin said that even though both he and his wife loved their daughters dearly, and remained affectionate to each other, their marriage was simply over. And his wife said that they were spending very little time together, and that Putin was devoted to his job so fully and absolutely that there was no time or space in his life for a marriage. There was not a single note of bitterness in Lyudmila's tone, in fact her expression throughout the announcement was of a warm enthusiasm. For those concerned, Lyudmila wasn't beheaded or confined to a monastery like the wives of Henry VIII or Ivan the Terrible. She seems to be thriving. Or at least this is what the Russian media wants us to believe.

As for Putin, he finally became unencumbered to fulfill the role of the husband of Russia itself.

Historically, all the other Russian leaders—from the tsars to Lenin and Stalin—were seen as Russia's stern but fair fathers or sometimes even as frail grandfathers (like Brezhnev in later years). The great change came with Gorbachev, a West-oriented, liberal figure who positioned himself as a cool uncle rather than boring father, which was met with either admiration or ridicule by the Russian population, or often with both admiration and ridicule. And then there was Yeltsin, who presided over Russia during the years following the dissolution of the Soviet Union.

Yeltsin further developed Gorbachev's liberal reforms, but the country kept experiencing unbearable political humiliations as well as being on the verge of economic collapse. Cultural elites were enjoying previously unimaginable freedoms—literature, film, media projects all flourished, journalists weren't afraid to speak their minds. But at the same time, the general population suffered from real poverty, just as the newly minted oligarchs kept appropriating the country's resources and flaunting their unimaginable wealth. Ordinary Russian didn't appreciate the freedom of speech and other tenets of democracy all that much. Most of them would have certainly preferred some stability. Yeltsin, with his flailing politics and boozy TV appearances came to be regarded as a weak alcoholic husband, the one that would flaunt his largess while drinking his wages away and draining the family's finances, a sadly familiar figure in many Russian households. Back then, a lot of people felt that Russia didn't have a chance to survive let alone regain power, unless it had a much stronger leader.

And just then Yeltsin unexpectedly resigned, and Putin took his place as acting president—a quiet, "faceless," seemingly unthreatening man who quickly established himself as a savvy, determined, and unusually ruthless politician.

There is an unconfirmed anecdote from Putin's first year in power that reveals his true character as a leader. The second Chechen war was going on, and there was no end in sight. The Russian Army surrounded Groznyj, the capital of Chechnya, yet the Chechen fighters refused to give it up. The only way to seize the city was to carpet bomb it. While the majority of the population had gone, there were still plenty of civilians stuck within Groznyj's walls, a lot of them elderly and disabled, tens of thousands or perhaps even hundreds of thousands of people. All of them Russian citizens. Top Russian military officials had an emergency meeting with Putin, still an acting president at the time, to assess the situation. One after another, seasoned generals would stand up and say that, no, the Russian Army couldn't possibly bomb Groznyj, when so many Russian civilians would be killed. And then it was Putin's turn to speak. He said: "We have to bomb it." There was a deadly silence in the room, after which everybody present understood that Putin was a true ruler of Russia and he was there to stay. Russian troops seized Groznyj soon after that, while razing most of it in the process.

Putin's ruthlessness allowed him to reestablish Russian power in all kinds of different aspects. He severely restricted the most vociferous oligarchs, imprisoning some while banishing others and appropriating their assets. He poured a lot of money into the Russian military, basically restoring its strength. He instigated some important reforms to help Russia's economy grow (rising oil prices didn't hurt either), which helped the Russian population emerge from poverty. But perhaps more importantly, he restored Russian national pride. In the eyes of the Russian general population, Putin "made Russia great again." Or rather, strong and scary again. And when he smothered new freedoms and silenced the opposition, the general Russian population didn't seem to mind.

The longer Putin stayed in power, the more Russian people came to associate him with an image of a brutal lover, or rather a brutal husband of Russia, the alpha male who would kill a whale, hunt a tiger, or soar into the sky with a flock of birds for his wife, but would not hesitate to beat some sense into her whenever needed. This image of a macho husband was in perfect sync with the movement to restore the old Russia's values that had been destroyed after the revolution of 1917, to reestablish the power of the Russian Orthodox Church, and create conditions for the general revival of Russian patriarchal traditions. In January of 2017, domestic violence laws were changed to make the punishment for offending husbands less severe. Before, a husband who repeatedly beat his wife would be sentenced to several years in jail. Now all he will get is a fine, which will probably hurt the family more than him, making the wives reluctant to report any violence whatsoever. It looks like it is only a matter of time before Domostroy, the infamous sixteenth century set of domestic rules, will be resurrected, along with the required tyrannical domination by a husband.

There is an old saying that is still uncomfortably popular in Russia: "He doesn't love you if he doesn't beat you." Which means that the only reason the husband wouldn't beat his wife is that he doesn't care about her. And it's obvious that beatings are done for the wife's own good. The saying suggests that the beatings are not just acceptable, but desirable, a symbol of marital attention and love. And this is precisely the type of husband that Russia got in the person of Putin. He does horrible things that often badly hurt Russian citizens, but the Russian population is okay with that. He is tough but sexy, he is full of care and love. Because, you know, he doesn't love you if he doesn't beat you. Here is how this logic works. The West applies sanctions against Russia. Putin's response is to apply his own sanctions that say "fuck you" to the West but actually hurt Russian citizens. The ban on foreign adoptions of Russian orphans is just one example. The ban on Western food import that is about to be followed by the ban on Western medications is another. The West is humiliated, the Russian pride is preserved. And so what if the Russian people would not have access to their medications and Russian orphans would have to rot in the badly managed state institutions?

He doesn't love you if he doesn't beat you.

The Russian opposition expresses discontent. Putin's government response is to violently suppress peaceful demonstrations and throw people into prisons, some of them seemingly at random. It's okay. He doesn't love you if he doesn't beat you.

Terrorists seize buildings, like the Moscow theater in 2002 or Beslan elementary school in 2004, and take hostages. Putin refuses to negotiate. He orders the attacks by the Russian armed forces, killing more than half of the hostages in the process (including small children). Two hundred and four hostages died in Moscow. Three hundred thirty-four died in Beslan, one hundred eighty-six of them children.

The deaths don't really matter, because Putin has shown to the world that the Russians are too tough to negotiate with terrorists. He doesn't love you unless he beats you.

In 2014, Putin annexed Crimea, which started an unofficial war with Ukraine, Russia's closest and historically most trusted neighbor. Many more Russian lives were lost. But the general population rejoiced—Putin managed to flip the West and regain some of the formerly Russian territories. It's uplifting, it's invigorating, it's sexy to have a leader who is making your country "great again."

So sexy it hurts. Really hurts badly.

DUTERTE
Nada in the Heart of Bluster

Ninotchka Rosca

Aꜰᴛᴇʀ ᴛʜᴇ 2016 Philippine presidential elections, Rodrigo Roa Duterte who emerged victorious was praised for having run a "perfect social media campaign"—seemingly a shrewd campaign tactic in a country where fifty-eight percent of the population is active on social media.[1] Examined dispassionately, however, this tactic was both inevitable and necessary, to create an "irreality," to transform into an icon of "change" a candidate whose only salient accomplishment was to maintain himself and his family in power for thirty years in a city ranked first in the number of murder cases.[2]

That "enhanced" digital narrative had all the elements of a telenovela—from thug-life rap imagery, mayhem, scatology, to a motley array of characters that was moved from the social margins to center stage: a soft-porn star, trans and queer people, dismally failed lawyers, and some cronies and members of the defunct Marcos dictatorship, left-wingers turned rightwing. These "sold" his iconography: a clenched fist, reminiscent of left militancy, but angled so that it was a full-frontal blow to the face of the beholder; Duterte himself cradling various over-sized guns and dubbed "The Punisher." Sound bites from Duterte both shocked and titillated, the equation of power and lust being one enduring machismo fantasy. He was also adept at using the "two-steps-forward-one-step-back" dance (or his handlers were), now admitting to having killed at least three people, now saying he'd never killed anyone; now threatening to slap his opponents, now lapsing into silence when they responded to his challenge. He showed his contempt (or non-knowledge) for critical issues facing the country, joking he would take a jet ski and plant the Philippine flag on the contested Spratly Islands—a non-stand which effectively sidelined one pivotal foreign policy issue. He was quick to use people's complaints without acknowledging his own participation in creating such problems, decrying, for instance, the loss of Muslim and indigenous land in Mindanao, despite the reality that the city he presided over for thirty years was a settler city, his own family having moved there from the Visayas, where his father had been a mayor in a round-robin system of power place-holding maintained by their relatives, the warlord Duranos. His bellows against such ills and on behalf of the afflicted were accompanied by the persistent claim that he had turned the city of Davao into the "safest" and most progressive city on earth—a lie unleashed by his trolls and picked up by media.

His fiercest opponent nowadays, Senator Antonio "Sonny" Trillanes, pinpointed this as the foundation of the supposed Duterte ability to bring change. The senator was upset that few challenged such an outright lie, enabling Duterte's campaign to build the mythology that safety and progress needed a strongman who could face down the criminal, the oligarchs, and, of course, the imperialists. Senator Trillanes himself had been intrigued by the man and had approached Duterte for a possible team-up at the start of the campaign. The senator's party had decided he should run for the vice-presidency, and he needed a presidential candidate to endorse. "I thought we would discuss policies," he said, "but all he did was talk about people he had killed." Not one to engage in a machismo slam dance, Trillanes and his party chose to endorse Senator Grace Poe—too precipitous a decision, as it would turn out, since that same afternoon, Mar Roxas, the standard bearer of the Liberal Party, which was in power, came knocking. "It was a few hours late," he said, "and, truly, Leni Robredo, who was not even in the list of names being considered, was fated to be the vice-president." Asked what he thought was the singular problem with the regime of Duterte, Senator Trillanes did not hesitate, "There is no core vision. There is nothing there to anchor policies—nothing at all." He added, "Except to secure and maintain power for himself. He has seen how vulnerable former presidents can be." The last two presidents of the Republic ended up in jail.[3]

It was a difficult election. A compound of both created and accidental opportunities, but what was most obvious yet studiously ignored was that only one of the four candidates was hostile to the clan and cronies of the late dictator Ferdinand E. Marcos. Enriched by his twenty years in power, clan and cronies had burrowed into the integument of the body politic for two-plus decades, preparing for a return to political power. Since the country had no provision for a run-off election should no candidate obtain a majority vote, the national electoral system was easy to game. The 2016 election had a three-to-one chance that a dictatorship-friendly candidate would win—which was what transpired. Duterte won, with a minority vote of sixteen million out of fifty million. One of his first acts as president was to declare, as he had promised during the campaign, that he would allow the burial of the late dictator Ferdinand E. Marcos at the Cemetery of Heroes—something opposed by nearly every president for the last thirty years.

Some things that Duterte said in his campaign that he would do, he did and he does. Some he tap-dances around. A lot he denies having said, though he would repeat what he denies saying. But there are dominant themes to his year-old administration.

The Imagination of Murder

He was sixteen years old, said a friend, when Duterte made his first kill; and when he told his family about it, to ensure their protection, he also said he "liked" it.[4] Recently, Duterte declared that he had "stabbed" someone to death when he was only sixteen or seventeen years old—which made me wonder about the rest of the story—that this was the start of troubles with his mother, Soledad. In his defense of the Marcos burial at the Cemetery of Heroes, Duterte had claimed that, his father having "stood by" the late Ferdinand, he could not abandon the Marcoses. Duterte's claim was not quite a lie but it was not true, either; his father had died in 1969, barely into Ferdinand Marcos's second and constitutional term as president and three years before he imposed martial law. There was nothing for Duterte's father to "stand by" at that time; lines would be drawn more firmly later on. But this statement about his father and the Marcos burial certainly was an insult to his mother. She had led the anti-dictatorship Yellow Friday rallies in the city of Davao in the 1980s. It was his mother who had recommended his appointment as Davao City vice mayor to the late Corazon Aquino, who had led the forces that overthrew the dictator. Now, here was Duterte, using his father to justify his decision to bury Marcos in the Cemetery of Heroes.

But Duterte also claimed to have been a student of and influenced by José Maria Sison, founding chair of the Communist Party of the Philippines (Maoist) or the CPP. One Mao quote then favored by Left activists of the era of the CPP's founding was "political power comes out of the barrel of a gun"—which Duterte appears to have taken to heart. But strength through killing was not used, in this instance, for the growth of revolutionary power but in the classic reactionary method of intimidation and removal of rivals, under the guise of solving criminality. This methodology Duterte brought to the national scene as soon as he became president. Using as justification an allegedly massive drug problem, murder was conducted by both an amorphous band of "vigilantes" and the police whose anti-drug operations racked up a ninety-six percent kill rate.

Duterte did say during the campaign that the drug problem would be his focus—and to solve it, he was prepared to kill three million Filipinos, even comparing himself to Adolf Hitler.[5] "I hate drugs," he would say again and again. *Drugs* and *kill* were the conflated ideas of his campaign—and since there couldn't have been that many drug pushers or "drug lords" in the country, the millions Duterte wanted to be killed were presumably addicts, occasional users, and small-time vendors. His election victory came in June 2016 and the killings started immediately. Barely a month into his victory, four hundred and forty people had been murdered.[6]

The killings were theatrical, the presentation of bodies calculated for maximum shock and fear. The killed were wrapped in packing tape, their humanity obliterated. They were tossed down back streets, under bridges, in vacant lots, in garbage dumps. Near them would be a crude hand-lettered sign saying, "Addict. Do not emulate." The killings occurred in the poorest sections of cities. About one in ten of the killed was female; but also LGBTQ people and, every so often, an activist or two. It was unprecedented in Philippine history. By the fourth month of Duterte's term of office, the kill rate had climbed to a thousand a month. Any criticism of this murder spree was met with a raucous digital chorus accusing the critic of being either an addict, who should be included in the presidential list of drug lords, or a drug lord supporter. A few murders were done for both the image of invincibility and ruthlessness. Albuera City Mayor Rolando Espinosa, for instance, had surrendered and elected to stay in a police jail for safety. On November 5, 2016, shortly before dawn, a team of policemen entered the precinct, disabled the CCTV, and proceeded to gun down the mayor, claiming he had "fought back." *Nanlaban* (fought back) would be a refrain in police operations where the kill rate approached one-hundred percent. A *Reuters* report noted, "Police have shot dead at least 3,900 people in anti-narcotic operations since Duterte took power in June 2016—always in self-defence, police say." One police station, Precinct 6, accounted for thirty-nine percent of the police-operation kills; its anti-drug unit was manned by police from Davao City.[7]

The supposed anti-drug campaign is named Operation Tokhang, from a portmanteau of the Cebuano words for "knock" and "talk." Critics have morphed that into "tok-tok" (for "knocking") and "bang" (for "gunshot"). There is a degree of irony in the use of a Visayan language by a president whose one appeal had been his having emerged from Mindanao, the largest islands whose indigenous and native population have been so dispossessed by various settler populations, a great number from the Visayas. Indeed, during one trip to Davao City, I was mistaken for a Maguindanao, one of the Muslim tribes, because I spoke Tagalog, which the Maguindanao supposedly preferred over any Visayan language common to the settler population.

The initial murders so unnerved the poor communities that tens of thousands "surrendered," banking on a government promise of "rehabilitation," which did not materialize. Instead, thousands were crammed into prisons meant to hold only hundreds, in a truly barbaric situation. Meanwhile, a billion-peso mega-rehabilitation facility—a donation from a Chinese person who had made his wealth in the Philippines (nobody asked how)—stood empty. The killed continued to pile up—up—and up; the last estimate by media and human rights groups placed the killed at more than fourteen thousand. Murder as a solution to a social problem had been so anathema to Philippine culture, with its bedrock values of *kapwa*, "togetherness" and "empathy," that a specific ritual and state of mind had to be created for killing—*juramentado*, a term that developed in the colonial period from the Spanish word *juramentar*, one who takes the oath.[8]

Implicit in these traditions was an acceptance of punishment, of being killed in the process of killing, so that balance was returned to the flow of human life. To be killed anonymously, to have no one held responsible, to not even have the murders investigated, and indeed to reward murder—these were so profoundly in violation of the national psyche that the nation cowered in the initial months of Duterte's murder spree. His digital army also poured forth a steady stream of accusations against the killed, labelling each murdered person an addict and labelling each addict a violent criminal. In the end, murder became almost a cursory by-product of even petty crimes, as it was the one crime not investigated and, moreover, perpetrated by state-sanctioned operatives and by the police who, at one point, launched an operation that killed eighty-seven in one week in what the police called a "one-time, big-time" operation. Most of the murdered were young men in Metro-Manila and four nearby cities.[9]

In a country where weapons were the preserve of the rich, there seemed no stopping the killings. Tatay Digong ("Father Digong," Duterte's nickname) morphed into Tatay Katay ("Father Butcher")—and because this is a culture of 150 languages, the first pushback would be the dirge rising from the country's poets and writers.

Tokhang

To this neighborhood where even houses are starved
Skeletons of thin plywood and ragged corrugated iron sheets
Where even the relic of rains gathered in potholes smells
Of grieving

They come, knocking on doors, polite as Power
Asking who are you, what do you do, where is this one?

And if this one is not there, asking who's there with you?
And if no one, saying, We think You'll do.
Because people here are a pack of cards—interchangeable
In life/unlife, breathing or not, laughing or weeping—
Shards of their not-to-be dreams glitter with
Sameness on intermittently washed skin—
Brown people, barefoot children, wide-hipped women
In tent dresses, printed with the yellow flowers
Of gardens they will never have.

Killing one hardly makes a difference
Even the houses starved to skeleton cannot
Be burned to permanent oblivion.

Yin/Yang

Overt machismo and its brother-in-arms, misogyny, are among the recurrent themes of Duterte's governance, with special animosity toward educated women in positions of power. A Freudian explanation can likely be found for this, considering that Duterte's favorite swearword, used liberally in his public pronouncements, irrespective of audience, is *putang-ina*, a combination of the Spanish word for prostitute (a practice unknown to native culture, hence the word borrowing) and the word for "mother" in many native languages. It is a many-layered word, denigrating of mothers even as it acknowledges the significance of one's links to the mother. The country itself is the Motherland, never the Fatherland. And strangely enough, Duterte sank to his knees, presumably in tears, beside his mother's tomb as soon as his election victory was announced.

Duterte sprinkles his public speeches with this swear quite liberally, irrespective of his audience. He also has a propensity to be scatological, to refer to his supposed sexual prowess or lack of it. It is both a casual and yet a serious swearword, the reaction to which can range from laughter to knives drawn. But it is a kind of nervous tic for Duterte, so pronounced that people have wondered if he has Tourette's syndrome. Coupled with his propensity to speak about Viagra, his sexual (non) prowess, his handful of mistresses, he has been suspected of being afflicted with coprolalia, perhaps the result of his being sexually abused, as he says, by a priest when he was a boy. Others see this as part of the full spectrum of misogyny that he employs to silence critics, similar to the virulent verbal abuse men's rights activists unleash on women and feminists. What is clear, though, is that he reacts very harshly and very intensely when a female contradicts him, even as some of his most anti-woman supporters are women. It is a symptom of the rather schizophrenic attitude toward women as a result of the clash between the values of indigenous and native cultures and the imposed cultures of colonialism and imperialism.

Senator Leila de Lima is probably the first political prisoner of the regime, jailed on allegations of drug trafficking involvement, though the government case against her has been revised again and again. The allegations are based on the testimony of convicted drug and murder felons, one of whom had to be nearly killed in prison before he would agree to appear before a congressional hearing. Unfortunately for Duterte's "swing to China" foreign policy, the felons' testimony also identified China as the main source of meth and the chemicals for meth production.

Here's a rather revealing chart from the Philippine Drug Enforcement Agency:

Foreign nationals arrested in the Philippines for meth-related drug offenses

January 1, 2015-August 12, 2016

China	49
Taiwan	13
Hong Kong	5
Nigeria	3
Japan	2
Korea	2
Liberia	1
Pakistan	1
Uganda	1

Source: Philippine Drug Enforcement Agency

But what offended Duterte was de Lima's opening of Senate hearings on the Davao Death Squad. As chair of the Philippine Commission on Human Rights, a constitutionally mandated institution, de Lima had dared investigate in 2009 a series of killings of petty criminals and street children in the city of Davao. Human Rights Watch had issued a report concluding that the killings were supported by the city government and detailing the existence of a Davao Death Squad (DDS—which would morph into Digong's Death Squad, that being the president's nickname and, during the presidential campaign, into Diehard Duterte Supporters, a standard presidential tactic of making light of any serious matter concerning himself).

President Duterte's response was terrifying, classic in the brutality of its tactics. At one point, he said she should just resign and hang herself. The barrage against de Lima and the Senate investigation was a virtual carnival of sadist misogyny. She was portrayed as a sexual outlaw because of a seven-year relationship with her driver. President Duterte said he had viewed a sex video of the senator, which had made him want to puke (the video never surfaced; what did appear was a porn video featuring a woman who very vaguely looked like the senator). Convicted drug-trafficking felons were summoned to testify at a congressional hearing to allege drug payoffs to de Lima. de Lima was eventually stripped of her Senate committee chair position and in due time, was arrested. She remains in jail. Meanwhile, the drug trade continues unabated and meth smuggling has spawned for the public a litany of names, most of them of Chinese lineage—plus the name of Duterte's son who was accused by Senator Trillanes of being a member of a Chinese triad.[10]

What caused Duterte's secretary of justice to finally admit that there was no sex video was the pushback from a women's group, a pushback that also became an organizing campaign. Every Woman launched a simple digital campaign, which trended rapidly; it asked women to post the simple statement "I am the woman in the sex video." I posted one, of course, finding this disempowerment of a woman by rendering her a "sexual outlaw" a familiar tactic. The hashtag #EveryWoman dominated social media for weeks—and eventually killed the story of the senator and the driver.

But this tactic of disempowering a woman by destroying her reputation would be used against Vice-President Leni Robredo—who became a target of rumors propagated by Duterte's troll bots, to wit, that she had a boyfriend, that she was pregnant, and so on. Duterte would himself allude to her looks, the length of her skirt

. . . Robredo, it would seem, deliberately maintains a public image that is in direct contrast to that of the president's. She is always polite, smiling, careful with her words, attends religious services, and is often photographed with the poor as part of her program of providing a livelihood for the disenfranchised. Duterte's supporters must know how threatening this contrast can be, and have resorted to calling her *lugaw* (porridge). Nevertheless, she has been subjected to some direct humiliation, being informed via a text message by a president's underling that she was no longer welcome to cabinet meetings. She immediately resigned her cabinet position and concentrated on consolidating her base. Recently, she accepted the position of titular head of the Liberal Party, the one remaining opposition party in the country. As some pointed out, the vice-president's duty per the Constitution is simply "to wait." And wait she does, speaking out sharply on a few issues, now contradicting the president and, rarely, supporting him.

Two other women in powerful positions are currently under siege by the Duterte regime: Ombudsman Conchita Carpio-Morales, who has opened an investigation into how 6.4 billion pesos worth of meth were smuggled at the Bureau of Customs, and Supreme Court Justice Maria Lourdes Sereno, who has consistently voted against the regime in cases brought before the court. Both had been appointed by the Aquino administration. Despite her nephew being married to the president's daughter, Ombudsman Morales opened an investigation into the Duterte family fortunes, upon the filing of information of the family's unexplained wealth by Senator Trillanes. Duterte immediately threatened to create an agency to investigate corruption in the Office of the Ombudsman. Morales's reply was succinct,

"Sorry, Mr. President, but this office shall not be intimidated. The President's announcement that he intends to create a commission to investigate the Ombudsman appears to have to do with this office's on-going investigation into issues that involve him. This Office, nevertheless, shall proceed with the probe, as mandated by the Constitution."[11]

Supreme Court Justice Sereno, on the other hand, is the object of impeachment proceedings in the Duterte-controlled House of Representatives, based on a complaint filed by a lawyer who is a member of a supposedly anti-crime organization, which seems to focus mostly on critics of the president. In response to the presidential spokesman's call for her to resign, Justice Sereno's lawyer said that resigning wasn't even to be considered an option. "As previously declared, resignation has never been an option. The CJ [Chief Justice] needs to face the impeachment proceeding precisely to preserve the dignity and independence of both the Supreme Court and the Office of the Chief Justice. She has done nothing to 'damage' the institution, and she has been doing everything to strengthen it," said lawyer Carlo Cruz, one of Sereno's spokespersons.[12]

Duterte's intimidation tactics had worked before on several of his male critics—but using such tactics on women who have likely faced a lifetime of intimidation is clearly not working. On the contrary, his pronounced dislike for intelligent women and pronounced liking for those who feed his ego—even with non-sense—contribute to a steadily hardening resistance to not only his policies but to his person as well. He could not have forgotten that it was a woman, now his ally, who survived a left-wing call for people's power to oust an incumbent president.

An Abstract Leftism

President Duterte had a leisurely eight months to consolidate control over the government and the nation, primarily through weak opposition the mainstream left offered. Beguiled by Duterte's claims that he was a "socialist," a "leftist" and could possibly consider a "coalition government" with the Communist Party of the Philippines (Maoist), this section of the political left in the Philippines carefully calibrated its responses. At the start of Tokhang, the New People's Army declared its support for Duterte's "anti-drug campaign" and even carried out a few operations against supposed drug suppliers. Eventually, as some activists were killed, the NPA withdrew its support. The CPP, meanwhile, continued its flirtation with Duterte, principally through the National Democratic Front's peace-negotiations team. Duterte rewarded the NDF with cabinet appointments—lucrative but not too powerful positions, from which they were ousted, nine months later, by the Congressional Committee on Appointments. Duterte washed his hands; it was not his decision, he claimed.

Did the CPP believe in its love fest with Duterte? The latter's tirades against the West—he used his favorite swear against then US President Barack Obama, threatened to cut diplomatic relations with Australia because it denounced his crude rape joke about a murdered Australian missionary woman, swore to end the Philippines' military agreement with the United States, and denounced a 1906 US massacre of Muslim men and women—were indeed astonishing for a country used to paying obeisance to the West. Even on the eve of his overthrow, the late dictator Marcos appealed to the US for help, not to any ideological opponent of capitalism.

On the other hand, the CPP has had a long relationship with Duterte in his city of Davao. A slew of photographs show him attending various celebrations of the NPA. The party knew him, not simply of him, and likely knew what he was—of the kind the party calls "bureaucrat capitalists," i.e., people who use government positions for capital accumulation. Marcos was one of them and his family continues the practice. The richest Marcos crony in Davao, who contributed seventy-five million pesos to Duterte's campaign in Davao belongs to the category. The former alliance between bureaucrat capitalists and the traditional landed gentry of the ruling class broke during the Marcos dictatorship. A struggle for economic dominance has been played out between the two reactionary forces, as the *bucaps* (bureaucratic capitalists) parlayed the capital gained through government corruption into control of mining, communications, cash crop plantations, power utilities, and technology. In the 2010 presidential elections, the CPP and its mass organizations chose to partner with one such bucap, endorsing Miguel Villar and allowing its legal personages to join the latter's senatorial slate.[13] That made for some awkward moments, as the Villar party included Ferdinand "Bongbong" Marcos in its senatorial slate. Villar lost to Benigno "Noynoy" Aquino III.

When CPP founding chair José Maria Sison said in a press interview that he would perhaps be able to end his thirty-year exile if the new president were *matino* (reasonable) like Grace Poe or Rodrigo Duterte, it opened the door for the rank and file to support either one, despite the supposed alliance of their political parties with Grace Poe. How much that statement turned the elections into a poll on Sison no one knows. When Duterte won, the country was rife with rumors that Sison would be at his inauguration. Bayan, the largest left formation, conferred the Gawad Supremo, named after the title of the head of the Katipunan which launched the revolution against Spain in 1896, on Duterte and Sison. Peace negotiations were reopened shortly thereafter.

Still, there had been bad omens. During the campaign, Duterte threatened "to kill" the KMU, the labor federation of the "national-democratic" left. He also attacked the National Democratic (ND) left's women's organization, despite its rather tepid response to his rape jokes. And though some activist community organizers and peasants were killed in the first months of Tokhang, the response from the ND left remained muted. Indeed, its human rights organizations kept a tally only of "political killings," keeping those killed in the anti-drug campaign separate. It would take some ferocious words from Duterte and the cancellation of peace talks to end hopes for a "coalition government." As if to drive the point home, fifteen NPA members were killed in the province of Batangas on December 4, 2017.[14]

Duterte was backed by some of the most reactionary elements of Philippine society, from the Marcos family to former President Joseph "Erap" Estrada whom the left had helped oust, from Gloria Macapagal Arroyo, who tried to imprison the ND left's people in Congress, to former President Fidel Ramos, a Marcos era holdover and very definitely allied with the US military. If this is so, why did the CPP amiably accept the Duterte candidacy? One hypothesis is that the ND left believed in Duterte's promises, because of their long relationship in Davao City. Another, which seems more cogent, posits that Duterte was the kind of brutal, power-hungry, and self-indulgent president needed to jumpstart the revolution from its long stasis. That is a kind of "Simon tactic"—it must get worse before it can get better—named after a character in the national hero José Rizal's novel *El Filibusterismo*. A third hypothesis says that the CPP has been reluctant to let go of the analyses that served as a framework for its struggle since the 1960s and that it has not taken adequate consideration of the emergent imperialisms in a multi-polar world. Hence, it continues with its attack on the Duterte-US regime, ignoring Duterte's growing dependence on loans from China, as his self-indulgence and his Tokhang deplete the Philippine government treasury. What is clear, however, is that the Philippines is once again, as in 1896, at the nodal point of powers contending for global dominance. How the Filipino people will conduct themselves this time could mean either dissolution or survival for a nation cobbled out of 7,400 islands and 150 ethno-linguistic groups.

By December 19, 2017, calling Duterte a "drug-crazed monster," the "country's number one terrorist," and a "madman," the spokesperson of the NPA's Merardo Arce Command said, "The revolutionary forces join the broad united front of all peace-loving citizens in the country to oppose and oust Duterte and install a government respectful of justice, genuine democracy, and freedom."[15] The lines were now drawn.

The Pushback Against Nada (Nothingness)

As Duterte's term staggered toward the end of its first year, opposition was beginning to congeal into a hard reality. The blatant incompetence of many of his appointees and the unabashed self-indulgence of his coterie—some two to three hundred are said to accompany him on state visits—merely underscored the lack of a core vision to his administration. Whether Senator Trillanes fully realized (and he likely does, which explains the ferocity with which he confronts Duterte) the meaning of his statement that nothing(ness) lies at the core of the Duterte governance, it is clear such nihilism can only disrupt and break, not create. The degree of stability forged since the overthrow of the dictatorship, no matter how lurching it has been, enabled the archipelago to rebuild its economy, pay back the loans looted by the Marcos clan and cronies, and reinstitute means of governance destroyed during his one-man rule. It may not have gone far enough in terms of democratization—economically and politically—but the current recurrent shock and awe tactic of Duterte's governance is a far cry from it.

Palpable evidence of how the policy of *nada* has been so terrible is the destruction of Marawi City, the only visibly Muslim city of the Philippines. While the rebellious Maute Clan allied itself eventually with ISIS, at least nominally, Duterte's volatile handling of the Moro issue—now vowing to pass the Bangsamoro Basic Law which would give them self-governance, then conveniently forgetting it; now calling the rebellious Moros his friends, and then abruptly threatening to eat their livers—undoubtedly turned the conflict acute. No one now can foretell what will happen in the area.

Duterte's supporters try to fill in the nada at the heart of his bluster, offering federalism, Constitutional change, and mass indoctrination through the *barangay* (village) councils, which are new organizations formed under the duress of Tokhang and in expectation of reward. Crowds of people are transported or made to transport themselves hither and yon—to call for national martial law, or federalism, or a revolutionary government, or even for the fraudulent promise of a distribution of the Marcos wealth. What is clear is a search for a vision that is absent, as Duterte takes the axe to the institutions of governance which, even to the paltriest degree, enabled some checks and balances. He warps the media, calling those who wouldn't toe the line "fake news" even as his troll bloggers parlay a plethora of fantasy; he has transformed Congress into a rubber stamp, dominated by some execrable personalities; he swings at the Office of the Ombudsman and the Supreme Court, miring them in chaos and controversy; he has purged the national police and filled the gaps with his "Davao boys," and now attempts to bribe the Armed Forces of the Philippines with a one-hundred-percent increase in base pay.

None of these will enable the nation as a nation to survive. All his political moves have been simply to eradicate opposition and to strengthen provincial warlords—to what end, no one knows for certain. Mainly to keep himself in power, even as the currency plummets to its lowest value in eleven years and the balance of trade suddenly shows a deficit. There is reward and punishment aplenty in the Duterte government—largely based on flattery or what he calls "loyalty." A newly appointed chair of the Dangerous Drugs Board made the mistake of saying that a billion-peso drug rehabilitation facility was useless. The president made the chair resign immediately. A congressman whose own party became so disgusted by his antics in defense of the president that they disowned and expelled him is the new presidential spokesman. The least taken in are the women who are familiar with how batterers maintain control and eradicate the self of the battered.

As the anti-drug campaign showed its essence as nothing more than a killing spree, the initial shock turned into outrage. The spark was provided by a nineteen-year-old, the son of an overseas worker who was brutally killed by fourteen motorcycle-riding "vigilantes"—the foot soldiers of Tokhang. He had no criminal record and was simply closing the small family store when he was abducted, taken to an isolated area, and beaten. He was then told to run and the poor young man couldn't, because of his clubfeet. The assassins mauled him and broke his arm before shooting him dead. His mother, arriving from Kuwait, unleashed her grief with the declaration that she had to kiss her employer's feet three times to be allowed to fly home and attend to her son's burial.

With nearly ten million working overseas, this kill had a resonance that went far and deep. The country hasn't managed to contend with its guilt over this semi-slave trade and the sale of women, and an untoward incident toward a female overseas worker taps into an abiding anger. The Catholic Church, which had been diffident in its dealings with President Duterte, decided to ring its bells for ten minutes for forty days in mourning of those killed in the "drug war." September 21, known as the day the late Ferdinand E. Marcos imposed martial law on the country way back in 1972, was a day of rallies and marching and assemblies. By November 1, the Day of the Dead, thousands of candles were being lit for the Murdered of the Duterte Regime, which had earned for itself the ND left's traditional denunciation of being linked to US imperialism.

Meanwhile, the BPO call center global industry, fifty percent of which the Philippines hosts, employing nearly a million workers, was at a standstill. Tourism was down. South Korean business was quietly closing its tent, following a case of extortion and murder of one of its managers in an incident designed to evoke the utmost repulsion: the policemen not only killed him but had the body cremated and the ashes flushed down the toilet. Nihilism creates its own unbearable cruelty. And the responding anger is equally unbearable.

Pact

Hoping to make a friend of him, you danced—
Knock-kneed, pot-bellied and nostrils-flaring—
With Death.
Hoping to stave off your own expiration date
Giving him instead
The toddler
The girl
The boy
The young man
The father
And a pregnant mother
Or two.

Death laughs with bloodstained teeth
Sending its most ferocious of worms
To feed on their anguish, pain and tears
So each worm will spend days
In orgiastic delight
When they all turn to your flesh.

NOTES

1   ABS-CBN News report, citing Digital Global Overview, January 25, 2017.

2   "Murder Rate Highest in Davao City—PNP," citing Philippine National Police statistics, *Philippine Star*, April 2, 2016.

3   Taped interview with Senator Antonio Trillanes, by author, New York City, July 20, 2017.

4   Confidential conversation with a journalist who has covered Duterte's political career. Duterte later made the claim himself while speaking to a Filipino expatriate group in Vietnam, on November 10, 2017.

5   "Philippines' Duterte Likens Himself to Hitler, Wants to Kill Millions of Drug Users," Reuters News, September 29, 2016.

6   "The Kill List," *Philippine Inquirer*, July 7, 2016.

7   "How a Secretive Police Squad Racked up Kills in Duterte's Anti-Drug War," Reuters Special Report, December 19, 2017.

8   Isagani E. Medina, "A Historical Reconstruction of the Juramentado/ Sablallah Ritual," *Anuaryo/Annales: Journal of History*, Vol. 11, No. 1, 1993.

9   "How The PNP's One-Time, Big-Time Operations Work," *Rappler*, August 27, 2017.

10   "Trillanes: 'Dragon-like' Tattoo Links Paolo Duterte to 'Triad'," *Philippine Inquirer*, September 7, 2017.

11   "Ombudsman Insists on Constitutional Duty to Probe Duterte," *Rappler*, October 1, 2017.

12   "Resignation Never an Option for SC Chief Sereno," *Rappler*, October 1, 2017.

13   "Capitalist Villar Is Communist Party's Bet for 2010," GMA Network News, December 24, 2009.

14   Delfin Mallari Jr. and Jodee A. Agoncillo, "NPA: 15 Dead in Batangas Were Ours," *Philippine Daily Inquirer*, December 4, 2017.

15   Zea Io Ming Capistrano, "Reds Vow to Overthrow Duterte," *Davao Today*, December 19, 2017.

ABOUT THE CONTRIBUTORS

Vijay Prashad is the executive director of Tricontinental: Institute for Social Research. He is the author or editor of several books, including *The Darker Nations: A Biography of the Short-Lived Third World* and *The Poorer Nations: A Possible History of the Global South*. His most recent book is *Red Star Over the Third World*. He writes regularly for *Frontline*, *The Hindu*, *Alternet*, and *BirGun*.

Eve Ensler is the Tony Award-winning playwright, activist, and author of the theatrical Obie Award-winning phenomenon *The Vagina Monologues*, published in forty-eight languages and performed in over 140 countries. Ensler is founder of V-Day, the twenty-year-old global activist movement to end violence against women and girls. Her play *The Fruit Trilogy* opened in 2018 with the Abingdon Theatre Company at the Lucille Lortel Theatre.

Danish Husain is an actor, poet, storyteller, and theater director. He has appeared in a number of films, including *Peepli Live* (2010), *AnkhonDekhi* (2013), *Newton* (2017).

Burhan Sönmez is a novelist, editor, and the translator of William Blake into Turkish. In 2018 he was awarded the first European Bank Prize for Literature for his novel *Istanbul Istanbul* (OR Books). A board member of PEN International, he won the Disturbing the Peace Award from the Václav Havel Library Foundation in 2017.

Lara Vapnyar came to the United States from Russia in 1994. She is the author of the novels *Scent of Pine* (Simon and Schuster), *Memoirs of a Muse* (Pantheon), and *Still Here* (Hogarth) and two collections of short stories. She is a recipient of a Guggenheim Fellowship and the Goldberg Prize for Jewish Fiction. Her stories and essays have appeared in *The New Yorker*, *The New York Times*, *Vogue*, *Harper's*, and *The New Republic*.

Ninotchka Rosca is a novelist and journalist. Her two novels—*State of War* (1988) and *Twice Blessed* (1992)—are considered classics of modern Philippine literature. She co-wrote José María Sison's *At Home in the World*, a book about the founding chairman of the re-established Communist Party of the Philippines.

O/R **C**

Cypherpunks
Freedom and the Future of the
Internet
JULIAN ASSANGE with
JACOB APPELBAUM, ANDY
MÜLLER-MAGUHN, AND
JÉRÉMIE ZIMMERMANN

When Google Met Wikileaks
JULIAN ASSANGE

Kingdom of the Unjust
Behind the U.S.–Saudi Connection
MEDEA BENJAMIN

A Narco History
How the US and Mexico Jointly
Created the "Mexican Drug War"
CARMEN BOULLOSA AND
MIKE WALLACE

Beautiful Trouble
A Toolbox for Revolution
ASSEMBLED BY ANDREW BOYD
WITH DAVE OSWALD MITCHELL

Bowie
SIMON CRITCHLEY

Extinction
A Radical History
ASHLEY DAWSON

Black Ops Advertising
Native Ads, Content Marketing, and
the Covert World of the Digital Sell
MARA EINSTEIN

Beautiful Solutions
A Toolbox for Liberation
EDITED BY ELI FEGHALI, RACHEL
PLATTUS, AND ELANDRIA
WILLIAMS

Remembering Akbar
Inside the Iranian Revolution
BEHROOZ GHAMARI

Folding the Red into the Black
or Developing a Viable *Un*topia for
Human Survival in the 21st Century
WALTER MOSLEY

Inferno
(A Poet's Novel)
EILEEN MYLES